Small Farm Equipment

Jon Magee

The Farmer's Library
Greenfield, Mass.

ISBN-10: 0985577401
ISBN-13: 978-0-9855774-0-7

Contents

Introduction

The primary goals of this book are to be straightforward, accessible, and useful, and I will be brief whenever possible.

I have assembled these topics to be relevant to small-scale farmers and to new farm employees, or anyone who has not had exhaustive hands-on training in the care and operation of small equipment. The set of skills and knowledge I've tried to encompass is one major facet of farm work, a facet that is poorly represented in the available literature. I wished for a book like this one when I started farming myself but found none. Visit an old extension library, however, and you'll find a good handful of books like this one, all from the first half of the twentieth century, the last time the small farmer dominated the rural American landscape. My hope is that this book will contribute in some small way to the success and prosperity of small farms in the new century.

I intend this book as a quick introduction to mechanical concepts and practical know-how, to accompany on-farm training or stand on its own. The text begins with a general discussion of acquiring, owning, and caring for equipment. There follows a section on the elements and terminology of mechanisms, and an illustrated summary of shop tools and their uses. There is a brief list of tips and guidelines for working in the farm shop, followed by a run-down of the most common maintenance and troubleshooting tasks. The last section describes the most common small equipment, with more specific tips for operation, maintenance, and troubleshooting. The discussion of tractors is brief, covering mainly safety and operation topics: a discussion of tractor maintenance is beyond the scope of this volume. The appendices offer bits of information which did not fit neatly into the text itself, including an outline for a safety discussion. The publisher's website will offer other handy information, including material originally intended for the printed text. I encourage you to visit and have a look.

There are many attitudes you may take toward operating machinery, but a healthy relationship with your equipment will eliminate many frustrations and much down-time. In this context, a healthy relationship means balancing your expectations with the capacity of the tools you're using. In the best case, a farm machine will give you years of faithful service, injure no one, and enjoy easy, regular maintenance.

When I discuss maintenance schedules or best practices here, I present an ideal, the best of all possible worlds. The mayhem of farm-life often creates scenarios less than ideal, situations which are unsafe for people or damaging to equipment, caused by favoring expedience over patience. I am not expecting this pattern to end, because life will never be perfect, especially on a working farm. However, it's all the more important that managers and employees alike be aware of ideal working standards so they may strive to achieve them and all the while be aware of any risks they may be taking.

What equipment offers

Machines can offer plenty of speed and productivity when they are well-tuned and operated properly, and when they are suited to the task at-hand. Thus machines can also offer labor savings at the bottom line. In the best of scenarios, they will free up labor to be spent where it is more needed, or simply reduce overall workload.

Machines can offer different ways to approach a task, allowing work to continue when conditions seem unfavorable.

Machines can also produce a lot of noise, smoke, fumes, and danger to life and limb. They can also quickly botch up a task, or rend themselves apart, with a hefty bill for repair or replacement.

What equipment requires

Machines almost always require a capital investment. Compared with labor, which is a slowly-accumulating cost, equipment often requires an up-front investment for its purchase. However, there is the slowly-accumulating cost of equipment, as well, in the form of maintenance, upkeep, and depreciation.

Machines require genuine effort to be operated properly and to perform up to expectations. This effort goes into choosing the right tool, learning its ways and workings, paying careful attention while operating, and knowing when a machine needs care.

Machines require responsibility. Keeping your workplace safe for yourself and your coworkers means having proper, comfortable safety gear and committing to its use. A day's activities may need shifting around if it's unsafe for coworkers to be near a certain piece of equipment in operation.

Your owner's manuals will have plenty of information on regular maintenance routines. However, I have the idea that all of these maintenance tasks can become familiar more through a readable guide such as this than through a brief owner's manual. So this guide is mostly generalized concepts which will help you know what a manual is suggesting you do. Then, when you read the manual for specific recommendations, it will be easy to follow.

Disclaimer

If your operator's manual, local or federal regulations, or your own good judgment differ from the information I present here, each of those sources should supersede this book. The present volume is too general in its scope to account for all possible circumstances. This advice applies to all questions of safety, management, maintenance, repair, and operation.

4

Concepts:

Equipment & Tool Management

Preservation and Tool Life

Living organisms need maintenance the same as machinery does. We're familiar with the activities which sustain our bodies—eating, drinking, resting, and all the more discreet and automatic processes by which we renew and heal damaged tissue.

With simple farm machines, there are few maintenance activities which are automatic. So while our bodies discreetly and subtly maintain themselves in spite of wear from use, machinery requires regular attention to stay functional and preserve its useful life. Neglect of this point will spell an early grave for a piece of equipment. Given the expense and difficulty of the mining, refining, and manufacturing that went into a tool, long life for a tool is good for the business and good for the environment. Spreading the initial cost of a machine over a longer useful life generally means more return on investment. Delaying the need to purchase new equipment means fewer items need to be manufactured. Furthermore, the labor cost of repair and maintenance is of direct benefit to your employees or your mechanic shop of choice, rather than to a distant manufacturing plant.

The longevity of a piece of equipment is mostly a function of regular care and maintenance. The maintenance activities described later in this book are nuts-and-bolts sort of scheduled tasks: they are straightforward, they are frequently needed but rarely done, and they provide the greatest benefit for the least effort. However, the biggest single maintenance task is just *management*. What's entailed in managing a farm's equipment?

Read the user's manual. At least one person should read each manual on the farm and be able to distill important points for other potential tool-users. Most commercial-grade equipment requires more de-

liberate upkeep than your average home ap-
pliance, and manuals contain critical information about maintenance schedules, proper
tool use, warranty information, and
troubleshooting. It's easy to get into the good
habit of reading manuals, and it doesn't take
long. The benefits of this practice can't be
emphasized enough.

Keep a maintenance log for each piece of equipment. Farm work
is hard on implements, and they need regular attention. There's no
way to know what maintenance needs to happen if the last maintenance was not recorded, so a well-kept maintenance log will save a lot
of worry. Simplify the scheduling process by making a copy of the
maintenance schedule for each piece of equipment and keeping it with
the log for reference. The various logs can then be kept in a binder for
protection, together with other relevant information. The appendix
contains a sample of my own maintenance logs, which can be down-
loaded from the website and adapted for your own use.

Plan ahead for equipment maintenance. Scheduled maintenance
will usually include changing fluids, cleaning or replacing filters, lubricating grease points, checking belt condition and tension, and so on.
These tasks are ongoing. Tasks which are performed as necessary—maybe once or twice a season, or more often as conditions require—are cleaning the fuel system, checking and re-gapping spark
plugs, sharpening blades, and so on. Equipment manuals often cover
each of these topics with instructions suited to the exact model, but
the Regular Maintenance section of this book offers an introduction to
the most common tasks.

The general theme of regular, preventative maintenance tasks is
keeping a machine clean, cool-running, well-lubricated, and properly
adjusted.

An engine's interior must remain very clean all the time. Dust,
debris, and even small animals can enter an engine through fuel or
through the air intake, and these things will all disrupt the delicate balance of fuel and air in a working engine. A clean fuel system and a
clean air intake, both of which should exclude foreign contamination,
will provide the optimal mix of fuel and air, prevent build-up within the

engine from less-than-complete combustion, reduce fuel consumption and emissions, and prevent unnecessary wear and tear.

All combustion engines generate excessive heat, and an engine without an effective cooling system is likely to get too hot. Some engines are liquid-cooled, meaning they have a radiator and fan to disperse their heat. Other engines are simply air-cooled, with fins and air inlets to allow heat to dissipate from the engine block directly. In either case, if there is an obstruction of heat transfer—if the radiator is covered in dust, or if an engine has lost its coolant, or the grille is covered in straw or grass clippings, for example—then the heat will remain in the engine, raising the temperature out of the safe working range.

Lubrication allows an engine's closely-machined, tight-fitting metal parts to slide across each other freely. When properly lubricated, an engine's parts never directly contact each other, but are separated by a microscopic layer of lubricant. Without oil or grease, metal rubbing on metal will generate friction and heat, resulting in serious deformation.

Equipment straight from the factory has been carefully tuned to its optimal working state. Vibration and wear from use will naturally affect the workings of a machine, and these workings must be readjusted to stay functional and efficient. For example, clutch pedals, brake pedals, and throttle linkages all have an ideal range of motion, and each linkage includes easily adjustable elements to stay within that range. Take a moment to look and you will see just how adjustable your equipment's workings are.

A machine which passes its life clean, cool, well-lubricated, and well-tuned will maximize its utility and value.

Certain small chores which are good practice but are rarely considered can also help keep a tool in good order for the long-haul. For tools and implements which are unpowered and might lack a detailed user's manual, these chores are all the more important in maintaining useful life.

General cleaning

Soil and debris are not directly corrosive, but they can hold moisture. Bare steel which is kept in contact with moisture will rust, so regularly cleaning off dirt and debris can help keep the rust down. A natural- or wire-bristle brush, a garden hose or pressure washer, or compressed-air tools might be appropriate according to the cleaning task. Also, keeping metal parts off of the dewy ground or out of the weather will help reduce or eliminate rust.

Also make sure that any fuel cans are free of dust or sediment inside, or else this will work its way into an engine and block the fuel system. Swish around a bit of clean fuel (same type as the can usually holds) to rinse out the can. Discard the small amount of contaminated fuel in a safe way. Never use water to clean a fuel can.

Oiling

A light rub-down with used motor oil or any number of commercial lubricants is the best defense against rust on bare metal parts during long periods of disuse. On the farm, one should be careful to use only food-grade lubricants on parts that might contact food or the crop bed. Such lubricants can include mineral oil or food-grade machine oil.

Sharpening

Many tools and tool parts benefit from a regular, careful sharpening, mower blades in particular. Sharpening is a skill worth developing. The tools for sharpening range from small hones and sharpening stones to grindwheels and angle grinders, all depending on the delicacy of the blade and how much metal has to be shaped.

A word of caution, though: overzealous or improper sharpening can shorten the life of tools, and occasionally cause bigger problems. For example, if the blades on a mower are not evenly sharpened, they will run out of balance and quickly wear out the bearing they are mounted on. Take the time to learn good sharpening techniques, and take your blades to a professional as appropriate.

Appropriate Tool Use

Proper use of a tool is key to ensuring long, useful life for that tool, but how do you know a tool's limits?

Manufacturers will often give enough information or instruction on the use of a tool to give a good idea of its ideal working conditions. They may even provide videos of their products in action. For PTO-driven implements, there is almost always a placard stating the maximum RPM at the PTO, which will give you an idea of the implement's working limit. A manufacturer may also be able to provide guidance through their technical support.

There may be professional training sessions available for some equipment, especially heavy equipment like forklifts. Some state extensions and other organizations will host training programs on safety and other equipment-related topics. Agricultural extensions, other organizations, and individuals will often post videos to the internet offering brief introductions to tools and equipment.

Fellow farmers are an excellent resource, as well, especially since many tools simply require exploration and even small modifications to make them work just right. An acquaintance who has already taken the time to become familiar with a given tool can make an excellent teacher. That said, there are plenty of farmers who abuse their equipment, so one can't assume unquestioningly that others' methods are always the best.

Really, you are your own best teacher in using a tool. Do not disregard the manual or any of the resources just mentioned, but do take the time to become familiar with the tool yourself. If a piece of equipment feels like it's running out of control, go slower. If it's making a funny noise, something might be wrong. With time and experience and close attention, you can get a feel for how tools like to run and what sort of loads they can handle.

When tools are used properly, they are at their most efficient and productive and their down-time and cost of repairs is least. Likewise, they are the safest to operate within their intended range. This will extend the life of the operator, as well as that of the tool.

Safety on the Farm

The most important element of a farm's safety program is communication, beginning with employee training. Every employee should have the chance to absorb the information and guidelines that will insure their safety and health, so take the time to communicate directly with everyone on the farm. Keep safety placards clean and visible, so everyone concerned can see them. I include in Appendix A an outline of key points for a safety training.

After training, communication must continue: if a vehicle or implement is in need of repair, mark it clearly to keep others from using it: flagging tape, a large sign, anything will do so long as it's obvious what it means. Remove the key from the ignition, as well, if there is a key. If you're an employee, make sure your supervisor knows the equipment is down and in need of repair—otherwise it may not be ready for action when it's needed again, resulting in frustrations for everyone.

Keep an ongoing dialogue among all the users of equipment: it's helpful to know if an implement is running roughly or differently from usual, so that problems can be identified as they arise. Two heads are usually better than one when it comes to troubleshooting machinery issues.

Safety gear

First of all, wear the right clothing for your work. In farming, at almost any scale that includes equipment, this means boots, sturdy pants, and a belt to keep your shirt tail in. Most farmworkers know that loose or frayed clothing can get caught or pulled in by machinery, but take a moment to check what's hanging off of your person: a length of your belt, a drawstring, a ring of keys? Even beyond entrapment injuries, loose clothing can cause you to trip or prevent your free movement in case of emergency.

Have the right safety equipment. The safety gear you purchase should be of high enough quality that it doesn't interfere with your work and thus discourage use. For those who only need safety gear occasionally, disposable gear is acceptable. If you're a daily or weekly user of this gear, re-usable gear is well worth the cost in comfort and ease of use. Take the time to figure out how to be comfortable in this gear. Make sure other people are using the appropriate gear, as well. This can include the following:

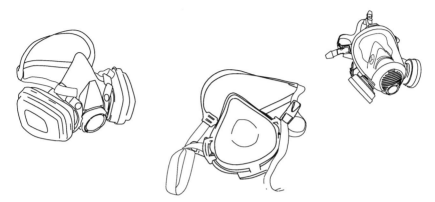

Respirators, from L: half-mask cartridge respirator for vapors and fumes plus dust; re-usable N95 dust mask; less common is the full face respirator for vapors, fumes, and dust with eye protection, a good option when goggles are uncomfortable with a separate respirator.

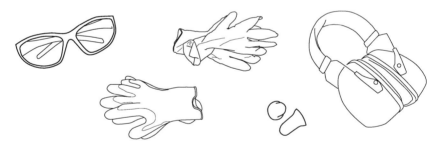

From L: impact-resistant glasses (or goggles for dust and vapor protection); sturdy work gloves; latex or nitrile gloves for oils and chemicals; disposable foam earplugs; earmuffs.

Be aware that N95 masks only filter out airborne particles, so if you are working around glue vapors, paint, or gas fumes, use a cartridge respirator for organic vapors (VOCs) *and* good ventilation. If you can still smell the fumes inside your respirator, you're not protected. Replace cartridges as necessary.

Nitrile gloves will keep gas, oil, and many other chemicals from penetrating your skin—these chemicals and their additives can make you sick in the short- and long-term. Rubber gloves are very inexpensive, available in varying thicknesses and cuff lengths.

Worn-out or dirty safety gear is its own kind of hazard. If glasses are so scratched that you cannot see clearly through them, they are no longer helping you. Expired respirator cartridges are no longer filtering out pollutants—if you can smell or taste a chemical, you are not protected. If your hands smell like fuel or oil at the end of the day, your skin has been compromised.

It can be hard to see the immediate value of money spent on good safety gear, but long-term hearing loss, retinal damage, or skin cancer are easily avoidable with the right safety gear and routines.

Some other items should be kept handy for use as needed:

First aid kits

Large fire extinguishers

Eyewash bottles or an eyewash station

Orange hand cleaner for grease and oils

Shop rags

Oil absorbent for spills

It is federal law that everyone is entitled to a safe and healthy workplace, so this safety gear must be freely available to all employees working near hazards. Take the time to warn and educate others nearby about hazards and offer them safety gear. Also take the time to arrange your work area so that others are minimally compromised. *Respect others' rights to a hazard-free workplace.*

Work with your environment

Just about every oil or fluid that comes out of or goes into equipment is hazardous to the environment, and we are required by law to contain and properly dispose of all such fluids. This includes gasoline, diesel, engine oil, hydraulic oil, transmission fluid, antifreeze, solvents, and lubricants. Almost all oils (including diesel but not always including gasoline) can be disposed of easily at waste oil collection centers, such as auto shops and transfer stations. Antifreeze (green or orange) must usually be taken to a transfer station or other waste disposal service. There is usually a small fee for oil and fluid disposal, but this can be negotiated sometimes for small amounts.

Avoid spilling any fluids on the open ground or in your shop. Keep a fair amount of spill absorbent on hand in case of emergency—readily available at hardware stores, though dry sawdust or kitty litter can also work. You may not be allowed to throw away absorbent with chemicals in it, so you may have to take it to a waste disposal service. Waste no time in cleaning up a spill—the longer you wait, the more seeps into the ground.

The best strategy is to avoid spills in the first place: make a plan before you make a mess, and place buckets, drain pans, or other containers to catch fluids. Use wire to hold small containers in awkward or tight places, and use funnels and tubing whenever necessary. Keep all containers and tubing for shop work clearly marked, and never use those containers for other farm tasks.

Any pile of oil- or solvent-soaked rags can spontaneously combust. Heat from oxidation builds up within the pile, raising the temperature above the oils' flash point and causing a fire. Promptly wash rags by hand with a strong grease-cutting dish soap. You may choose to burn them, if local regulations allow.

Batteries of just about all kinds should be kept out of landfills. Lead-acid (vehicle) batteries, NiCd, NiMH, Li-ion, and many small consumer batteries are required by law to be recycled to remove their heavy metals—lead, nickel, cadmium, lithium, and mercury. Transfer stations, auto parts stores, hardware stores, and various other outlets offer battery collection bins. Many recyclers ask that you discharge all power from the batteries before recycling, if possible.

General safety guidelines

Always be alert, and never act in haste. Avoid doing too many things at one time. It's easy to feel rushed by the day's work, but your health and that of others is far more important in the long run.

Turn engines off before you attempt to work on them or inspect them. It may be necessary to let an engine cool before performing work, to avoid burns. Use parking brakes and chocks to keep equipment from rolling. Use jack stands (**not jacks**) to keep implements firmly held up before crawling underneath. Keep brakes and other safety mechanisms in good working order—just because a vehicle *can* run without these parts doesn't mean that it ever should.

Never run an engine indoors, even idling, without proper ventilation, as this will quickly cause a carbon monoxide hazard and end in suffocation. Mechanics use high-temperature hoses to direct exhaust outside, if they must run a vehicle in a garage. If you are using machinery in a greenhouse, open all the doors, raise the sides, or turn on the vent fans.

If you farm in an arid area, your small equipment is almost certainly required to have spark arrestors on the exhaust. This simple, inexpensive element prevents stray engine sparks from starting wildfires. Check with your local dealer if you're unsure whether your equipment has an arrestor.

Be diligent, and hold yourself and others accountable for good practices.

Acquisition and Budgeting

At the simplest level, deciding on whether to buy a machine or not comes down to comparing two situations: life without the machine, and life with the machine. What is the cost for completing a task without this machine? Is that cost greater than the cost of completing that task with the machine, plus the ongoing costs from purchasing and using the machine? Are their other things to consider, such as quality of life?

These questions can be hard to answer. A piece of equipment good for general use around the farm is the easiest to justify, because of the many benefits it could potentially bring to the bottom line. However, this general usefulness also makes it hard to quantify the benefit of the equipment.

A highly specialized piece of equipment is easier to assess, since it fits neatly into a given category of operations. Suppose, for example, that you are considering a mechanized onion-topper. The cleaning of onions is generally a brief, limited activity each season, so it is easy to determine what the total labor cost of cleaning onions by hand is. You can then compare this labor cost with an estimated cost for the same activity with the onion-topper, and then further determine how long it will take to recoup the cost of purchasing or renting the topper. If your gross sales of onions are too small a fraction of the machine's cost, then it will take many years to reap the full financial benefit from the purchase. Conversely, if your gross sales of onions are many times the cost of the machine, you might consider a model with higher capacity.

If you are new to making significant capital expenditures for your farm business, you will want to speak to an experienced farm accountant or an extension agricultural economist to discuss depreciation and the tax write-offs available to farms and other businesses. A reduction in your business taxes may make a significant difference in the final cost of a purchase to you.

A further question is whether cash flow or available financing can accommodate the expense. The cost of labor slowly accumulates over the length of a task, while the cost of a machine is one big shot at the outset, followed by a much slower accumulation of operation and repair costs. The cost comparison becomes complicated by the question of financing costs—is labor being paid out of a line of credit? Is equipment financed?

Yet another question is whether a purchase makes sense right now. If you are considering a serious upgrade in equipment, then the benefits in productivity are probably the most important element of the decision. However, if you are simply replacing equipment with more or less equivalent goods, you can view your farm equipment not just as individual items but as a succession of investments over decades. If you replace equipment too frequently, you may spend more on equipment over the long run. If you replace equipment too infrequently, you may spend more on repair and on the costs of down-time over the long run. The right timing of purchases will make best use of the value of your current equipment while not overly delaying the benefits of newer equipment.

Finding Information

Many frustrations arise from following misguided advice (or no advice at all), so it is important to know who is available to help you get the most out of your equipment.

First, there are the official dealers who sell and service equipment, and who also sell the parts to maintain and repair that equipment. If you are unsure of the nearest dealer to you, visit the manufacturer's website and find out. Having a friendly relationship with a good dealer is mutually beneficial—you benefit from their expertise and they learn more about their equipment's field performance. If your nearest dealer isn't to your liking, find another nearby.

Secondly, there is your local or on-farm mechanic. Some mechanics are happier to make farm visits than others, so ask other farmers in your area who their mechanic is. In certain very agricultural areas, it can be easy to find repair shops with plenty of relevant experience. In many places, though, the best farm mechanic might be another farmer. Unfortunately, they are often busiest at the time you need them most. Some automotive shops will do work on farm equipment, as will most rural machine and fabrication shops.

The manufacturer itself can be an excellent resource. Some manufacturers are more available for service and support than others, but if you have a persistent problem which dumbfounds your dealer and mechanic, the manufacturer might be your best hope.

Agricultural extensions are not often focused on equipment issues, but there are notable exceptions. Extension personnel can also probably point you to other resources, if their own resources fall short of answering your questions. Agricultural engineers are few and far between here in the Northeast, but the few we have are excellent and highly knowledgeable. Other regions' extensions may be better-staffed.

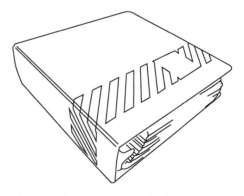

There are a handful of books and publications which can be

A typical service manual binder.

helpful. One useful book will be the official service manual for a given piece of equipment. This is separate from the owner's manual, when available, and contains detailed instructions on maintenance and repair. There are also many books more detailed than the present volume, offering walk-throughs on more advanced repair work. An excellent education can be culled from certain industrial supply catalogs—from their pages one can learn what unfamiliar parts are called, what off-the-shelf replacement parts are available, and all sorts of other interesting information. Favorites include McMaster-Carr and Grainger, both of whom also have good websites for browsing.

The internet occasionally offers some good information in text and in video form. Wikipedia has many excellent explanations of different types of engines and mechanisms.

Appendix D continues this list of sources for further information.

Your local machine shop

If you are unfamiliar with the work of machinists and fabricators, I'd like to summarize their role for the farm. Machinists are metalworkers who specialize in cutting and tooling parts—mostly mechanical transformations. Fabricators specialize in construction and repair by welding. The two specialties often co-exist in the same shop, though many shops will specialize in one or the other.

All the metal machinery you have was fabricated and machined by some shop somewhere. Plenty of agricultural equipment originates in small shops, although plenty of it originates on large assembly lines, as well. Often times certain parts of an implement will be from specialty manufacturers, then a small shop will assemble the various parts onto a frame of their own making.

On a local level, machinists and fabricators do primarily custom work. For this reason, a complex job can become quite expensive for you, the customer, but in certain cases this is entirely justifiable—especially when something has to be done, and you lack the time and proper equipment to do it, or when a custom implement will greatly enhance productivity.

More automotive-oriented machine shops will specialize in standard automotive tasks, such as resurfacing heads on motors, resurfacing cylinders, or rebuilding alternators and starters.

On the farms I have worked on, we have used machine shops for various jobs: reinforcing and straightening cultivator sweeps no longer commercially available, refurbishing electric motors, making custom seeding plates for a vacuum seeder, repairing aluminum irrigation pipe, and building custom packing-line equipment. If you have large pieces of metal or sheet metal which would be hard to cut with your own tools, a machine shop has equipment to do so quickly, safely, and accurately. Your local machinist/fabricator is your ally in making your equipment work better for the way you want to farm.

Just as importantly, though, your local machinists and fabricators are an excellent resource. If they are willing to take the time to chat with you, they have a wealth of knowledge about how machinery works, how different metals perform, and how best to go about repairs. In the process of explaining to them what job you would like them to do, they might tell you how to do it cheaply yourself.

Some welding shops or individual welders also offer portable welding services, which can be very useful for a farm—on-site welding means you don't have to haul bulky projects such as irrigation pipe to another location.

Concepts:
Mechanical Elements and Terminology

Power Generation

Power generation, as a term, refers to the part of a machine that provides power to the moving or working parts. For most farm equipment this means a motor, usually either gas, diesel, or electric.

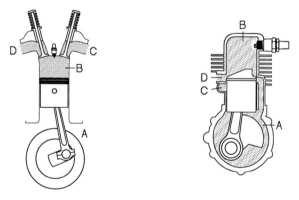

Four-Stroke Engine   **Two-Stroke Engine**

A. Crankcase; B. Cylinder (combustion chamber); C. Intake; D. Exhaust.

Gasoline (Gas) engines are simply those engines that take gasoline as their fuel for combustion. The fuel is ignited in the cylinder by the spark plug, providing the engine's power. **Two-stroke engines** take their specialized lubricating oil in the fuel itself. The oil is mixed with fuel because the fuel mix passes through the crankcase on its way to the combustion chamber, and the crankcase must be lubricated. These

with modern implements. The output shaft on other, non-tractor engines may also be referred to as a PTO.

Sprockets are toothed wheels which interface between shafts and chains. The most common types of chain on the farm are **roller chain** and **flat chain**.

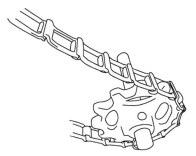

Sprocket for roller chain, with keyway for keyed shaft.

Sprocket with flat chain.

Showing the parts of roller chain.

Two gears, with teeth in a 'herringbone' pattern.

Gears are toothed wheels which interface between shafts and other gears.

Pulleys are wheels which interface between shafts and belts. The most common belts are **V-belts** and **multigroove belts**, although you will occasionally see **round belts** and **ribbed belts** on farm equipment. Belts are said to run in the *sheave* of a pulley.

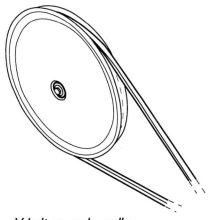

V-belt around a pulley.

Bearings are mechanical parts which bear friction from rotation. A **plain** or **friction** bearing is simply a fixed collar which supports a shaft. **Ball bearings** and **roller bearings** can bear much more weight and speed because they support the shaft with freely rotating balls or rollers. These bearings may be permanently sealed, or they may have a channel for taking lubrication. Ball and roller bearings are often mounted in so-called **pillow blocks** or **flanges**. Bearings should be replaced if they cease to allow free rotation of a shaft. Running equipment with bad bearings will often result in damage to other parts.

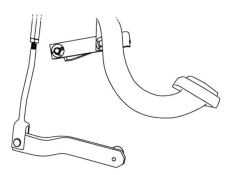

The visible parts of a clutch pedal linkage.

A **linkage** is a series of mechanical parts—levers, shafts, and so on—connected in chain-like fashion to transfer movement. All foot pedals and control levers on a tractor operate linkages which reach back to the systems they control. When a vehicle or implement is new from the dealer, all of these linkages have probably been tuned just right. However, almost all linkages on equipment are adjustable, because as parts wear from use or as vibration loosens joints, the linkages must be adjusted to compensate. Look for turnbuckles and adjusting nuts, bolts, and screws when a linkage wanders out of its ideal range, and follow the standards in your operator's manual for checking that range.

Lubrication

Lubrication is the use of fluids or powdered solids to reduce friction between contacting parts. Common lubricants are various greases, oils, silicone sprays, and—for dry lubrication—powdered graphite. There are many types of lubricants for many different applications. White lithium grease is a common all-purpose lubricant for standard medium-duty applications. Higher speed or higher operating temperatures will require other grades, often denoted by their different colors. Light lubricants such as WD-40® or PB Blaster® can penetrate tight, seized areas, but lack the sticking power of something as thick as grease. Graphite is useful as a dry lubricant, often sold by tractor dealers and auto part stores.

Non-toxic lubricants are important on parts that may contact food or leak near food-grade surfaces, and a bottle of mineral oil (often sold as a laxative) can be easily obtained from a pharmacy for this purpose. Commercial food-grade grease and food-grade machine oil are available at a price, but their labels should be carefully read for limitations on food contact.

How much grease should you use? The rule of thumb is to keep pumping grease into a zerk until it starts to peek out of the joint that's being lubed. Then you can be sure that the interior of the joint is full of grease. If you pump too much, wipe away and dispose of any excess—you don't want stray grease getting where it doesn't belong.

A zerk in detail.

Grease fittings, or **zerks**, are small ports which accept the grease from a grease gun. It's important to be aware of the locations of all the zerks on your machinery and make sure they are greased at regular intervals. Owner's manuals will give recommendations for how often particular zerks need grease. A grease gun's aperture must point straight into the zerk's grease fitting, or else grease will spill out the side as it is pumped. Be sure to wipe dirt or dust off of a grease fitting before pumping, or else you will drive that dirt into the mechanism itself. If a zerk is not accepting grease readily, it can be easily replaced: unscrew the stubborn zerk and thread a new one in. It's a good idea to have a standard assortment of replacement zerks on-hand. There are also hand tools for unclogging zerks with pressure.*

It is occasionally appropriate to wipe down a wear-surface with grease directly, if there is no zerk.

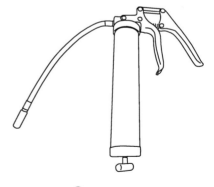

Grease gun.

* Note that zerks occasionally need a breather plug to be opened before they can accept grease. This is not often the case, but a manual will point out such cases when they occur.

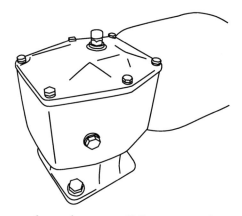

A **gearbox** is an enclosed case, housing a set of gears and filled part-way with gear oil. The case is sealed to keep the oil in and to exclude debris. There are usually three plugged holes in a gearbox: the drain plug, the fill level, and the filler hole.

A gearbox on a flail mower, where the PTO shaft transfers power to the gears, then to the mower head. Note the vent on top, and the level plug on the side.

Engine oil refers to the oil circulated throughout an engine to lubricate its workings in the crankcase. In small engines, there may simply be a reservoir with a combination fill hole/check port and no oil pump. In more complex engines (such as those on tractors and vehicles) there will usually be an oil reservoir with a drain plug, an oil pump to circulate the oil, a filter to clean particles from the oil, and a separate oil fill cap atop the engine block. See the Regular Maintenance chapter on how to perform an oil change.

Fasteners

Fasteners are hardware used to bind parts to each other. Most familiar are screws and nails, but there are many kinds for many purposes. Nuts and bolts in particular have many different specifications, ranging from the hardness of their metals to the size or *pitch* of their threads (usually given in threads per inch, *tpi*).

The hardness of a bolt is indicated by markings on its head. Three radial lines identify the common Grade 5, for general use. Six radial lines signify Grade 8, a much harder bolt for more strenuous applications. Metric bolts will have numerical markings on their heads (8.8, 10.9, 12.9), also referring to their hardness. Note that **shear bolts**, which are *designed* to break away as a safety feature, should be no harder than Grade 5. Shear bolts should always be tightly fastened with a stop nut, or else they may not break cleanly and quickly.

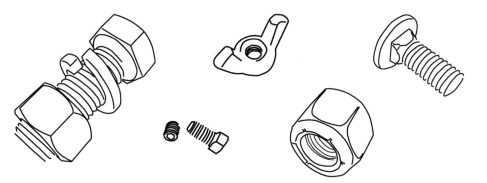

Above: selected fasteners: Top, from L: Hex bolt with split locking washer and hex nut; wing nut; carriage bolt. Bottom, from L: hex-drive and square set screws; stop nut (with nylon ring inset).

Bolts and and their complementary nuts and washers are all referred to by the diameter of the bolt shaft, not by the size of the bolt head—so the nominal size of the bolt won't tell you what size wrench to use on it.*

Rivets are another means of fastening, requiring their own specialized tools, and they can be useful where a joint will be at least semi-permanent. Rivets are easily set but have to be drilled out to be removed.

Cotter pins are very common for retaining parts on a shaft. They are slipped through a hole in the shaft and then splayed out to stay in place.

Hitching and Towing

Hitch pins are used to hitch trailing wagons and implements to a vehicle. Pins for use on a tractor's three-point hitch are referred to by their 'category,' according to the table below. A 'category 2 lift arm pin' would thus be 1-1/8 in. in diameter.

* Refer to Appendix B for a table of bolt size to wrench size.

Category	Tractor HP	Top Link Pin Diameter	Lift Arm Pin Diameter
0	Up to 20	5/8 in.	5/8 in.
1	20 to 45	3/4 in.	7/8 in.
2	40 to 100	1 in.	1-1/8 in.
3	80 to 225	1-1/4 in.	1-7/16 in.
4	180+	1-3/4 in.	2 in.

All pins on a three-point hitch (or any type of hitch) should fit as snugly as possible: if you're fitting a small pin into a larger lift arm, use a bushing to fill the gap. Always make sure the pin-to-lift-arm or pin-to-top-link connection is secured with an **R-clip** (hairpin) or **linchpin** sized to completely fill the hole it rides in. The security of all these connections relies, by design, on the strength of the pins to resist shearing forces. A pin that is loose in a hole can easily be bent rather than sheared, such that an implement can come loose and create a hazard for people and equipment alike.

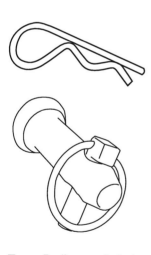

Top: R-clip or hairpin. Bottom: linchpin, well-sized to the hole in the lift arm pin.

There are various types of towing hitches. Most common on tractors is the drawbar with drop pin, and most common on vehicles is the ball hitch. Be careful to make use of all the safety features available with any type of hitch. When towing heavy equipment on a trailer, use chains (not straps) and tie-downs to secure them. Ratchet the chains down in opposing directions—pulling forward in the front, and backward in the back—until the equipment's rubber tires are visibly compressed against the trailer deck and all slack has been worked out of the chain's length. Make sure there's no corner around which the chain can move and slip loose.

It is worthwhile to note that most loads tend to ride forward, as the force of braking is much greater than that of accelerating, so plan accordingly. Never exceed the towing capacities of a vehicle, hitch, or trailer.

Tools for Maintenance

The purpose of this section is to help you choose the right tool for your task. I was humbled once by a comment from a neighbor, as I used my multi-tool to fix a tractor's fuel line—"Son, you must be a farmer, cause it looks like you've got every tool but the right one."

Take time to do a job with the right tool, and you'll probably save time in the end; you'll also probably be happier with the result—parts un-damaged, tools intact, and fingers neither skinned nor smashed.

Files are used for sharpening blades and edges, for removing burrs, for smoothing out surfaces, and so on. They come in a variety of shapes (here, **round** (1) and **flat** (2)) and sizes and degrees of aggressiveness to suit a purpose. They must be cleaned out regularly during use with a wire brush in order for them to be effective.

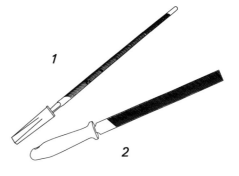

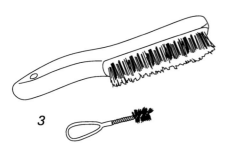

Wire brushes (3) are one option for cleaning metal surfaces, especially grooved or uneven surfaces. The bristles can be any of a variety of metals for different purposes. A wire brush is generally only useful if its bristles are straight and clean, so if you gum up the bristles with old grease, try using a solvent to clear it out. These brushes come in a vari-ety of shapes and levels of stiffness.

A **bench grinder** (4) is a powered wheel that sits on a workbench or table for sharpening or grinding away metal. A variety of different wheels are available in different grits and different materials. Also available are wire-bristle wheels and buffing/polishing wheels.

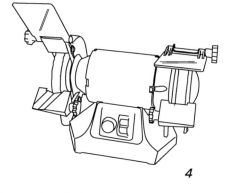

4

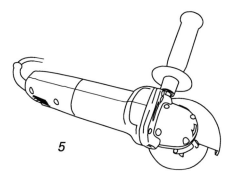

5

An **angle grinder** (5) is a hand-held power tool which takes different types of wheels for cutting, grinding, abrading, and polishing metal. If you have not used an angle grinder before, heed the safety warnings and seek out instructional materials.

Punches (6) are used to knock out frozen pins or bolts. **Center punches** have a point for marking a spot for drilling or other machining. **Cold chisels** (7) are used for chipping and chiseling, and differ from the cutting chisels used for woodwork. All of these tools are used with a hammer.

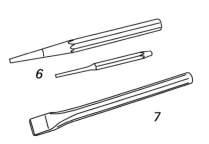

6

7

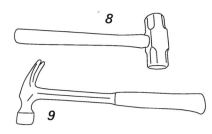

8

9

There are various types of hammers for different tasks. **Sledge hammers** (8) are most useful for shop work, given the broad face and greater heft of the head—these are the hammers you would use for punches and chisels and general heavy hammer work. **Claw hammers** (9) are the more familiar carpentry tool, better for driving and removing nails while framing construction. **Rubber** and **wooden mallets** are non-marring, as are some soft-faced metal hammers.

Note: I have to mention that hammering, while an important action, is not often the solution to a problem. If you find a task is requiring serious wailing with a hammer, think twice about how else you could achieve your ends. Heating of parts with a torch, dousing with lubricants or diesel fuel, use of leverage, use of a gear puller or press, even just careful reconsideration of the problem—these are all strategies which will either ease the job of the hammer or make it unnecessary. In either case, the hammer is the tool most likely to disfigure a seized part and cause further frustrations.* Find ways to reduce the damage done by your hammer blows. Definitely do not use other tools (*e.g.*, wrenches) as hammers.

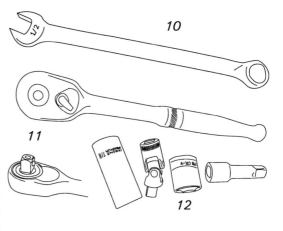

Wrenches do all sorts of good work, when matched to the task. Most familiar are **combination wrenches** (10), which are open on one end and closed on the other. **Socket wrenches** (11) are matched to ratchet drivers to speed the work of fastening. **Sockets** (12) come in metric and SAE (imperial) sets, with standard or deep wells, in standard chrome finish or graded for use with **impact wrenches** (13) (a pneumatic tool commonly used in auto shops on wheel nuts). **Spark plug wrenches** are sized extra-long to fit over the whole body of the plug—these wrenches are often included with small equipment directly from the manufacturer, but some socket sets include deeper sockets for common plug sizes. **Adjustable wrenches** (14) are useful when you'd rather not carry around a large set of combination

* An old idea, phrased by Abraham Maslow: "I suppose it is tempting, if the only tool you have is a hammer, to treat everything as if it is a nail." It can take time to think through your non-hammer options, so be patient.

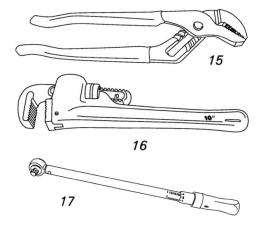

15

16

17

wrenches, although they do not always grip as nicely as fixed wrenches. **Channel locks**® (15) are a lighter-duty version of the **pipe wrench** (16)—both of these wrenches are designed to be used on pipe and tubing, since their teeth cut in to grab the metal of the pipe. Neither is suited to use on nuts or bolt heads, since they will deform the metal with their cutting teeth. **Torque wrenches** (17) are designed to direct a fairly exact amount of torque (meaning turning force). This feature becomes important when a part must be tightened just so—neither too loose, lest it come undone, nor too tight, lest its parts be damaged. Manuals will tell you when to use a torque wrench for particular fasteners by specifying an exact amount of torque to apply (in foot-pounds or Newton-meters).

Most types of wrenches have a preferred direction of rotation. In some cases, a wrench's grip and leverage will only be effective in the preferred direction—for example, pipe wrenches and channel locks have one-way teeth to grip parts. In the case of adjustable wrenches, turning in the proper direction reduces strain on the adjusting screw and preserves the tool's life.

Also, always start threading any bolt, nut, or fitting by hand and not with a wrench. Only once a part has started threading easily by hand should you continue with a wrench. Otherwise, the excess torque from a wrench can easily cause cross-threading and mar the parts. This is especially important when threading parts such as spark plugs—engine blocks are often made of soft cast aluminum, and their threads, once ruined, can be difficult to fix.

Filter wrenches (18) are designed to gently grip oil and fuel filter cartridges to safely tighten or remove them. Choose one or two that are appropriate to the size of filters you'll be removing. Sometimes

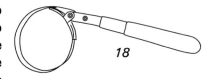

18

you can get away without a filter wrench, by which I mean you can sometimes just use gloved hands to get sufficient force. Don't try using other non-filter wrenches. Always thread-on a filter by hand to avoid damaging the threads on the filter mount, then follow the directions from the filter on how far to tighten it—usually some fraction of a turn past when the gasket makes contact or past hand-tight.

Drills are familiar to many, but there are various points worth mentioning. First, use a good, sharp drill bit suited to the material you're drilling—the right bit might cost more than you want to spend. There are guides available on the sharpening of bits, but there are also inexpensive, electric bit sharpeners now available from tool catalogs. Secondly, use **cutting oil** to lubricate the bit point when you're drilling into metal. Starting your hole with a center punch will help prevent the bit from walking. Also, try to match the speed of drilling to the size of the bit and the material being drilled. This be-

19

comes more relevant on a drill press when one can somewhat accurately dial in the speed of the drill. A **drill press** (19) is a drill fixed to a sliding shaft on a stationary pedestal to allow for precision drilling. **Hammer drills** are designed for drilling into concrete and masonry—many of the nicer **portable drills** (20) feature a hammer drill setting, though the feature is not usually as aggressive as a dedicated hammer drill.

20

Screwdrivers (21) are useful for more than simply driving screws, though I would recommend an actual **pry bar** (22) for prying work. However, for driving screws and general fastening work, I prefer **portable impact drivers** (23). These drivers add a hammering action to their driving when they meet resistance, greatly improving the speed of driving screws or nuts. They are also less likely to strip a screwhead than a

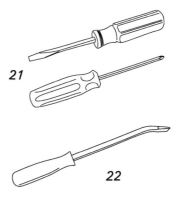

21

22

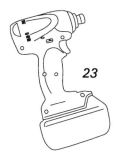

23

drill with a screw bit is. With the right bit adapters and sockets, these drivers can be used effectively on nuts and bolts.

Hacksaws are a type of handsaw and have various blades suited to cutting different materials, including metals. **Bandsaws** are powered saws which can be horizontally or vertically mounted. **Bandsaws** range from small to very large in size and capacity. These saws are excellent for cutting metal and plastic. **Abrasive cut off saws** are more aggressive for cutting metal, and do so by using an abrasive wheel rather than a blade. **Circular saws** are primarily intended for wood. **Chop saws** offer more precision when cutting wood, plastic, or light metal. **Demolition saws** (24) (such as the Sawzall®) are good for rough work—they accept a variety of blades, so they can work on wood, metal, and plastic.

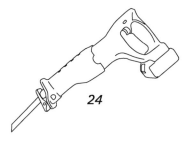

24

25

26

27

28

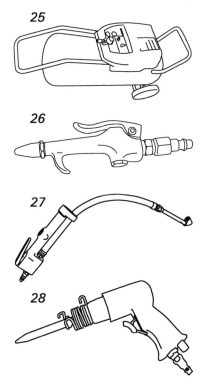

A variety of pneumatic tools work in conjunction with an **air compressor** (25). Simplest are **air guns** (26), which simply release the pressurized air for cleaning and drying purposes. This is the tool of choice for cleaning cooling fins, or for blowing out water lines. **Air chucks** (27) are used to inflate tires. **Air hammers and chisels** (28) can make short work of any seized part, but they are not precision tools. Straight and right-angle **die grinders** (29) perform a similar function as other grinders, but they are generally smaller and do finer work, accepting cut-off wheels, abrasives, and wire-bristle wheels. The aforementioned impact wrenches are valuable for large, heavy-duty nuts, but due to their great working force they can

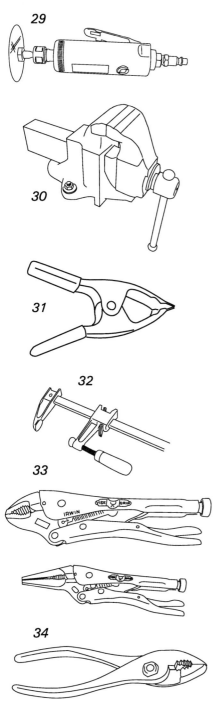

easily ruin threads or shear off a bolt.

The **machine vise or heavy-duty bench vise** (30) is probably the most useful vise for a farm workbench. It is heavy and durable and designed for metalworking, often with part of the vise useful as an **anvil**, as well. When setting up your workbench for the first time, take time to look up the proper bench height and vise placement.

Clamps are an important part of shopwork, given that they can often take the place of a spare set of hands. The simplest clamps are **spring clamps** (31), fine for holding together light work such as wood and plastic. **C-clamps, bar clamps** (32), and **pipe clamps** are good for applying significantly more holding force. **Vise-Grips**® (33) are locking pliers which come in a variety of styles, all useful as clamps. Similar to the Vise Grips are bench-mount **hold-down clamps,** such as you will often see mounted on drill presses and other machine tools. **Magnetic clamps** are a cheap, quick solution for welding jobs.

There is a wide array of **pliers** for many different tasks, but the most generally useful are **standard (slip-joint) pliers** (34), **needle-nose pliers** (35), and **lineman's pliers** (36). Standard pliers are the most familiar type—they have a 'slip joint' which allows the clamping width of the

34

jaws to be widened. Needle-nose pliers are useful for small work or tight spaces and include a light-duty wire-cutter. Lineman's pliers are designed for heavier wire and cable. **Bolt cutters** (37) are available in sizes from miniature to large, and, because of their lever action, they offer the ability to cut through thick or hardened metal bolts. (Above a certain size, though, it's much easier to just use a grinder or saw for this purpose.)

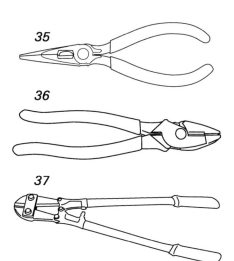

Some basic tools for electrical work include a **wire stripper/crimper** (38), **needle-nose pliers**, **wire cutters**, and **insulated screwdrivers**. A good **voltmeter** or **multimeter** (39) is critical to test and diagnose problems, as well as to ensure that a circuit you're about to work on isn't live. **DC meters** are good for equipment work, and **AC meters** are for circuits in buildings. The most common electrical tasks involve simple replacement of wires and cleaning or re-seating of terminals. For this reason, a **battery terminal cleaner** (40) for vehicle batteries is extremely useful, or just a wire brush. **Petroleum jelly** or a commercial **terminal protectant** will help prevent corrosion on a battery's electrical contacts.

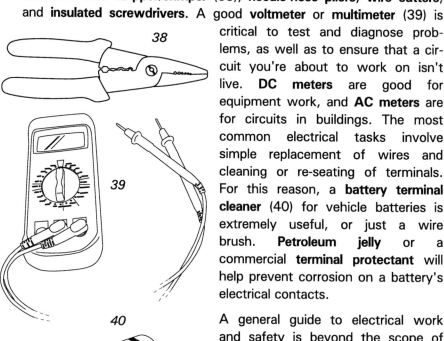

A general guide to electrical work and safety is beyond the scope of this work, but these guides are readily available. Check Appendix D for recommendations.

A **gear puller** (41) is a screw-type device which aids in removing gears, sprockets, pulleys, and so on, from their shafts. After the arms are set around the part to be removed, a center screw is driven either by a handle or by a wrench to slowly push the shaft out from the center of the part. The process is much more controllable than banging away with a hammer and punch.

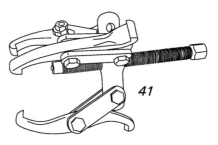

41

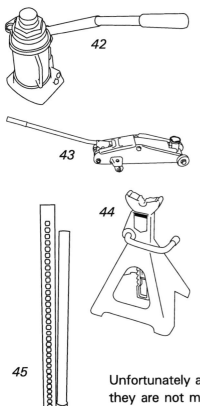

42

43

44

45

Jacks and stands are an important part of positioning work. Scissor jacks, such as come with most automobiles, can be useful, although **bottle jacks** (42) and **floor jacks** (43) are often more stable and rated for higher loads and are thus better for shop work. **Jack stands** (44) are very useful and significantly more stable than jacks—these stands are used to hold equipment up after a jack has raised the equipment. Then, once the stand is underneath, the jack itself may be removed and positioned elsewhere. **High-lift ratchet jacks** (45) (sometimes known as 'tractor jacks') are useful for their large range of lift—so if you must lift a high tractor axle from its 2-feet-from-the-ground resting position to 3-feet-from-ground to remove a wheel, this jack is the one for the job.

Unfortunately all jacks can tip or accidentally release, so they are not meant to hold loads over people. Use jack stands or ramps if you must crawl under raised equipment. Every time you prepare to crawl under a vehicle, assess the stability of your jack stands thoroughly before endangering yourself or others. Always use **chocks and/or parking brakes** to prevent rolling, and work on a hard, level surface, preferably concrete.

Work stands or **material support stands** are the equivalent of jack stands for bench work. **Saw horses** (homemade or otherwise) make a fine general-purpose substitute. Most important is that you not injure yourself or others with unsteady, unwieldy work pieces.

Taps and dies (46) are tools for cutting screw threads into drilled holes and onto shafts, respectively. These tools are sold individually and as kits. It's particularly handy to

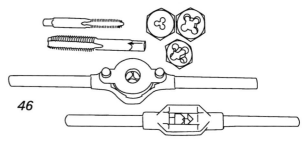

46

have a **rethreading kit**, which generally includes **rethreading taps and dies** (47) and **thread-cleaning files** (48). When you have a bolt or fitting which has damaged threads but would be hard to replace altogether,

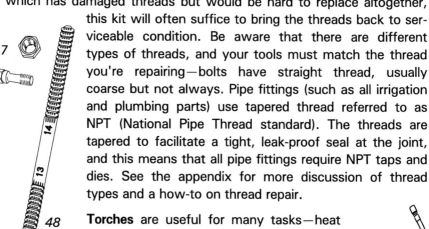

47

48

this kit will often suffice to bring the threads back to serviceable condition. Be aware that there are different types of threads, and your tools must match the thread you're repairing—bolts have straight thread, usually coarse but not always. Pipe fittings (such as all irrigation and plumbing parts) use tapered thread referred to as NPT (National Pipe Thread standard). The threads are tapered to facilitate a tight, leak-proof seal at the joint, and this means that all pipe fittings require NPT taps and dies. See the appendix for more discussion of thread types and a how-to on thread repair.

Torches are useful for many tasks—heat can help loosen seized parts, soften plastic and rubber tubing to more easily insert fittings, make disfigured metal malleable enough to reshape, and on and on. Choose your gas based on the task. **Propane** is the lowest heat, so a small propane torch is good for tasks which are delicate—if you're softening plastic tubing, for example, too much heat will simply melt the tubing and ruin the work. **MAPP™ gas** burns slightly hotter. Light-duty torches available from the hardware store are simply **fuel/air**

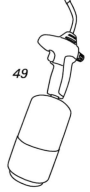

49

torches (49), which are safest and easiest for general work on a farm, and generally not hot enough for shaping metal parts. Fuel/oxygen torches, however, include a pressurized oxygen tank which considerably raises the flame temperature. Propane/oxygen is available, but most common for metal work is **Oxyacetylene** (50), which combines oxygen and acetylene gas.

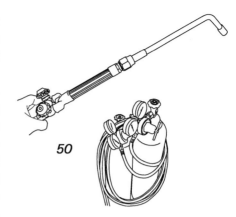

50

These torches have specialized tips for various tasks such as brazing, welding, and cutting. You should seek out professional training in the safety and proper use of oxyacetylene and other fuel/oxygen mixes. Be careful with all torches, even propane—do not use open flame near any flammable materials or vapors. Wear **welding goggles** or a **mask** appropriate for the task at hand.

Welding has a well-established place in the farm shop. **Stick welders** are historically most common on the farm, though **MIG** and **flux-core welders** are considerably easier to use. Seek out professional training before you choose a welding unit and before you attempt it yourself, as you'll need plenty of practice and guidance. Local community colleges and technical schools are excellent resources.

Tips for Shop Work

The following suggestions will help to make your time in the shop more productive, more comfortable, and safer for all concerned. These guidelines are just the basics, however, and over the years you will get a better feel for how you like to work.

Be safe. Wear protective gear.

Safety should always be first priority. No matter what kind of rush you might be in, nothing will stop work quite like an injury to yourself or another.

Take care of your safety gear: keep it clean by washing it, drying it, and storing it in plastic bags. No one wants to use dirty safety gear. Replace worn-out items in a timely manner, and always have enough for back-up.

It is federal law that everyone is entitled to a safe and healthy workplace, so this safety gear must be freely available to all employees working near hazards. Take the time to warn and inform others nearby about hazards and offer them safety gear. Also take the time to arrange your work area so that others are minimally affected. Respect others' rights to a hazard-free workplace.

Be aware.

The second part of safety is foresight. Don't crawl under equipment that might fall, nor stand behind equipment that might roll. If you must service a three-point hitch implement from below, raise the implement and set it down on jack stands—don't trust your safety to something as uncertain as a tractor's hydraulics.

Before you strike a hammer blow, consider whether anything might fly up and strike you back. Use clamps to hold down loose work pieces.

If you're unsure whether a given task is doable, don't start it unless you're sure you can halt at any time. Avoid getting caught in a dead end where the only way out involves injury.

Plan your workspace. Plan your approach.

Use good lighting. Portable work lights are inexpensive and come in all shapes and sizes.

Take time to clean up and clear your space before starting. Give yourself room to work and be comfortable. If you're going to be disassembling, leave yourself space to put parts down in an orderly way—this will help with reassembly.

A muffin tin is one excellent way to hold small parts in a clear order. Another option is taking pictures as you go, so you have a reference for how to put it back together. Use masking tape or a marker to make labels as you go and to show the proper orientation of parts. If you must remove an adjusting nut or screw, count how many threads are showing—this will save time and calibration when you're reassembling.

Gather all the tools and parts you'll need. Once you've disassembled a piece of equipment, its parts all strewn-about will be an obstruction to other activities. If at that point you have to order a replacement part, your mess will be an obstruction for as long as you must wait for the necessary part to arrive.

For small work, bring it up to a comfortable bench height. Work at the level you're most comfortable.

Keep all your work firmly affixed, either in a vise or on the workbench with clamps. This will make it unnecessary to ever saw, grind, or hammer anywhere near your hands or other body parts, and will prevent workpieces from becoming dangerously unstable.

Time your work appropriately. If you are repainting an implement in the winter, for example, you will have to do so in a heated, enclosed space, as paint requires at least about 60 degrees F to set properly. This can lead to a significant build-up of fumes indoors, and even if you yourself are wearing a respirator, the fumes can be unbearable for your coworkers. Paint in the spring or summer and you may leave doors and windows open with fans running.

Work with your body.

Use natural motions whenever you can—this goes with the oft-re-peated axiom of 'working smarter, not harder.' The weight of your body is an asset when your work is correctly positioned, so make your workbench the height of your midriff, no higher.

Use the right size of tool. Using a small hammer for a big job, for example, will lead to strain and overexertion.

Use leverage whenever you can, more so than brute force. A few long pieces of rebar and pipe are useful shop items for this purpose. These pieces can be used to extend the handles of wrenches and thus free up seized nuts and bolts with minimal effort.

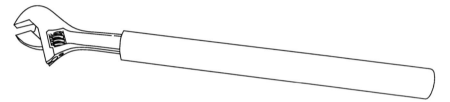

Consider your method.

If a method that you have chosen is damaging your workpiece, recon-sider. There is almost always at least one right way to perform a re-pair, without harm to yourself or your work, and this right way is worth finding out.

If you're adapting tools for a novel purpose, be aware of this fact. Pushing a tool past its limits can easily break the tool or the workpiece or create an unsafe condition.

Ask for help.

If you can't perform a task without physical strain, it's not worth doing yourself. Know your limits and respect them. You have to bear in mind the long-term perspective, and you cannot farm with a broken body.

If you simply don't know the best course of action, talk about it with others. Many qualified technicians live near you and many of them will speak with you for free or nearly free. Your co-workers might also have ideas you have not thought of, which are often worth hearing—regardless of their level of experience in shop work.

Regular Maintenance and Troubleshooting

Acquiring Parts

For a given piece of equipment, your operator's manual will often have part numbers for the most common items to replace—filters, guards, and so on. You can often find the part number printed or stamped directly on the part you're replacing—this is sometimes the only way to ensure that you'll be ordering the same part. Sometimes manufacturers have a complete parts list available online, but you can consult with your dealer or other service shop for getting replacement parts, as well. If they're doing the work, they'll be finding the parts themselves anyway.

Many generic replacement parts are available off-the-shelf. Spark plugs are a good example: there are many brands and it's easy to find equivalents between manufacturers. Many of the most popular brands of small engines have generic equivalents of their various filters, as well. It may not be necessary to follow the manufacturer's advice to the letter, which is generally to "Use only genuine _____ brand parts," even down to the engine oil. If you're unsure, though, work with your dealer or parts shop to find appropriate equivalents. If you're shopping online, be sure of what you're buying, and don't be too shy to ask for help in choosing parts.

General Notes

Oil and water should always be kept separate. For example, if a port is designed to take engine oil, never let anything else besides engine oil into it—no rain, coolant, fuel, and so on. If a fuel tank is meant to hold gasoline, never leave it open to incursion by rain, and never wash it out with water. Never let oil get mixed in with coolant—and so on.

Likewise, never let gasoline and diesel mix, as machines take either one or the other and never both.

Never let dust or debris into an engine or into an engine's fluids. Clean around any ports before opening them, to prevent dust from falling in. If you must walk away from an engine that's been opened up or has a cap off, cover it up or plug the hole with a clean rag.

Engine Oil

On a two-stroke engine (string trimmers, mini-tillers, chainsaws, and so on), the engine oil is mixed into the fuel. There is no separate procedure for changing engine oil, because the fuel mix itself serves to lubricate the engine. Two-stroke engines should be very obvious, be-cause they sport "oil and gas" placards and ratios for that mix (shown at left). If a piece of equipment has any of these signs, you must use an oil/fuel mix of the proper ratio, or the engine will quickly be ruined. You must also only use oil labeled for use with two-stroke engines.

Four-stroke engines (mowers, most tillers, vehicles, tractors, and so on) have an oil reservoir for lubricating the engine, separate from the fuel. It is the oil of these engines which must be checked and changed regularly. Do not run two-stroke oil/gas mix in a four-stroke engine.

Mixing gas for two-stroke engines

The goal of this process is to make sure that the two-stroke engine is getting a proper, consistent amount of oil per unit of gasoline.

1. Follow the ratio guidelines from the engine's manufacturer. If the manual or a placard on the engine says to use 50:1, that is the ratio to use. Some bottles of oil will suggest a leaner mix, but that has the potential to damage the engine. Use the implement manufacturer's recommended ratio.

2. The manual or the bottle's label will direct you in making the mixture by giving you an amount of oil per an amount of gasoline to achieve the desired ratio. Try to be precise.

3. First pour half the desired amount of gasoline into a clean, empty, dedicated two-stroke gasoline can (you can make a

clear label, or buy a brightly colored tag to mark the can as such). Next, pour the desired amount of two-stoke engine oil into the can. Pour the remaining amount of gasoline next. If you are not certain you're going to use this whole can of gas within a month, add an appropriate amount of fuel preservative, as well.

4. Put a cap on the gas can and shake vigorously for one minute. Before using a can of two-stroke gas mix that's been sitting around, give it another shake to make sure the mix is evenly blended.

Old, stale gas is one of the most common culprits when small engines won't start readily. Without a preservative, the gas formula will break down enough to cause real difficulties over time. A small bottle of preservative is a few dollars and goes a long way.

Checking oil on a four-stroke engine

This is a simple task, but critical, also. The engine oil in four-stroke engines prevents friction within a working engine from tearing the engine apart. Most manufacturers recommend checking oil levels before each use. Engines must be on a truly level surface to get an accurate reading. Sometimes one can simply remove a dipstick and take a reading from it; but other times, if the reading is vague or oil has splashed all over the dipstick, it must be wiped with a clean rag, reinserted into its hole, and removed again for a proper reading. Sometimes you will need to look very closely or use the reflection of light to tell where the oil is—if the oil is fairly fresh and clear it can be hard to see its level. Do not check the oil while the engine is running.

Because the engine oil and the engine's interior must remain very clean, it's important to wipe clean the area around the dipstick before removing it. Otherwise, dust and sand may get on the dipstick or fall into the dipstick port, thus getting into the engine.

Have you noticed any oily sludge around the engine? Identify and repair leaks promptly, and top up the oil. You can also lose engine oil if
it's pushed out by stray combustion gases (known as blow-by) or if
it's pulled up into the cylinder and burned away. These conditions are
common on older engines, and may require new piston rings or cylinder sleeves. Until the condition is fixed, you will need to add oil regularly.

If the engine oil looks odd, this may be the sign of a problem. Milky
(grayish) oil can be the sign of coolant or water in the engine oil, usually due to a leak inside the engine. Very thin oil may be due to fuel
contamination, likewise usually due to an internal leak. In either case,
prompt service is necessary.

Changing oil on a four-stroke engine

This is also a straightforward task, but it may require some fore-
thought. It's important to know when the manual calls for oil changes.
The first oil change is quite soon after an engine first sees use, often
after 5, 25, or 50 hours of operation—every engine is different. This
early oil change removes all the fine metal particles which are pro-
duced by the engine wearing in. All subsequent changes occur at a
longer interval.

1. To change the oil, first be aware that oil will drain much
faster and more fully if the engine has warmed up—so running
an engine until warm before the oil change is a good idea, since
this will help remove the old broken-down oil and its impurities
from surfaces within the engine. Take precautions not to be
burned by draining oil—wear protection or let the engine cool a
bit. The oil will be the same temperature as the engine block.

2. Determine the grade of oil to be used—compare typical use
to the recommendations in the manual. Here is an example of a
manual's oil grade chart (for reference only, do not base your
oil grade on this chart):

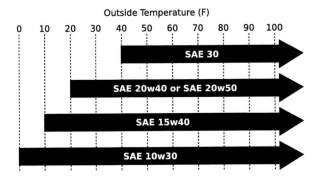

Outside Temperature (F)

3. Plan out how you can neatly collect the used oil from the drain plug without spill. This may involve jacking or lifting the equipment, with an appropriately-sized drain pan ready underneath or a can or bucket hanging by wire below the drainplug.

4. Remove the drain plug, and loosen the oil fill cap to remove any suction which might prevent the oil's draining. Let the oil drain until it's down to a very slow drip—the more you get out, the better. Tipping the equipment may be necessary to get all the pockets of trapped oil out.

5. Change the oil filter, if there is one, remembering to moisten the oil filter's gasket with a drop of oil on your (gloved) finger, and following the guidelines for how tightly to affix it.

6. Replace the drain plug, taking care to make it neither too loose nor too tight! It's almost never appropriate to use all your strength in tightening a drainplug if you have the proper choice of wrench.

A common error is over-tightening either the filter or the drain plug, and this can be a serious problem if the soft, aluminum threads on the engine block become stripped.

7. Pour into the oil filler hole a little less than the total recommended amount of oil. Give the oil time to trickle down into the oil pan (longer if the engine and ambient air are cold) then check the level on the dipstick. Add small amounts of oil at a time, waiting for the oil to trickle down each time, until the dipstick level reads full but not over-full.

8. Start the engine and let it run for a minute—this will get the oil well-distributed throughout the engine block. Check the level again and top up the oil if necessary.

Cooling System

Combustion engines run hot relative to the ambient temperature, but they have an ideal range of operation. Their design always incorporates a cooling system to carry away excess heat from the combustion. There are two types of cooling systems, air-cooled and liquid-cooled.

Cleaning air-cooled engines

The engines of small power equipment are almost always air-cooled. The cooling system on an air-cooled engines consists of a series of metals fins, designed to increase the surface area from which the engine's heat can radiate. These fins function only if fresh air is actively moving across them, directly contacting the metal of the fins. The primary task of maintaining this type of cooling system, then, is to keep the fins and air passages clean and free of dust, dirt, and debris.

Use a brush or, preferably, an air gun to clean cooling fins—an air gun will do a better job getting into corners and between tightly-spaced fins. Also make sure that any airways in a motor's cover are unblocked—these might be a front-end grille or mesh or just a series of vent-holes around the housing. Some engines, especially two-stroke engines, will require you to remove their plastic cover to access cooling fins on the flywheel and on the cylinder. Best practice is just to blow out any debris from anywhere around the engine.

Checking coolant on a liquid-cooled engine

Liquid-cooled engines use a 50/50 mix of antifreeze (glycol) and distilled water, so if you must refill a radiator or overflow tank, use only

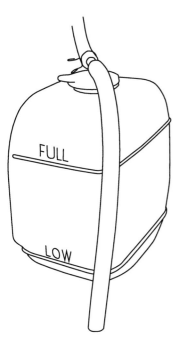

these two ingredients, only at this ratio. Check your bottle of antifreeze, though, to make sure it's not pre-mixed—many service stations are now selling 50/50 mix bottles for the sake of convenience. Using distilled water (as opposed to tap water or spring water) will prevent build-up of mineral deposits and corrosion inside the engine. Such deposits could block or restrict coolant flow, leading to serious engine problems, so stick to distilled water only.

When checking the coolant level, you have two places to look. First is the overflow tank. This plastic reservoir has two lines around the middle of its body, marked full and low. As the engine warms up, the coolant within it expands and overflows into this tank. Just check that the level there is between the full and low marks. If it's above the full mark, it will spill out when the engine gets hot. If it's below the low mark, top it up with 50/50 mix.

The second place to check is in the radiator itself. This can only be done when the engine is cool because a radiator becomes pressurized when the engine warms up, and hot coolant will spew out if it is opened. Twist off the cap and make sure the coolant reaches to within a half-inch of the top. If the level in the radiator is too low but the overflow tank is full, you may have a problem with the overflow-and-return mechanism, by which the radiator automatically draws coolant as needed from the overflow tank.

Cleaning radiator fins

A radiator consists of an array of tubing set into a block of tiny metal fins. Because these fins are so close together, and because the farm environment is so dusty, these fins must be cleaned out at least once a year, more often in dusty or hot conditions. Hot water from a hose works well, and there are various cleaners at auto shops to use with water. Another good tool here is an air gun, held within an inch or less of the fins, slowly passing over every square inch of the radiator. You

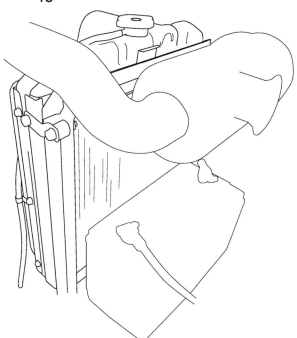

should work from both sides of the radiator, and keep going until no more dust spews out. The air gun's stream of pressure is very narrow, so you will have to make very narrow passes—broad swaths will be completely ineffective.

Whichever method you use, though, avoid flattening the soft radiator fins. You will have to bend them back straight with a radiator comb, otherwise.

A typical tractor's radiator, situated behind the battery and the air cleaner. The cap is on top.

Flushing coolant

Your operator's manual will give you a time-table for replacing the coolant in the radiator. If there is contamination in your coolant (for example, from a leaky head gasket), you may want to flush more often. To do so, find the drain cock at the base of the radiator. Place a bucket large enough to catch all the coolant underneath. Open the radiator cap and open the draincock, letting all the fluid drain out. Make sure the overflow tank is also empty. Take away the first bucket (or however many you had to use to catch the old coolant) and replace it with an empty one. Now run water from a clean hose into the top of the radiator and let it drain into the bucket until it runs clear. Let all the water out, then close up the draincock. Fill the radiator and overflow tank with a 50/50 antifreeze/distilled water mix. Run the engine long enough to let it warm up, then check the coolant level again and top up as necessary. You may need to bleed out any air bubbles introduced into the system, so consult your manual.

Hydraulics

Almost all tractors have hydraulic systems, though small power equipment generally does not. Tractor hydraulics power any lift arms on rear or mid-mount hitches, as well as any auxiliary ports. Often the hydraulic oil doubles as the transmission oil, so it's doubly important that the level be checked and maintained regularly. Check the level at least weekly, if not every time you use the tractor. Have you noticed any oily sludge sitting somewhere on the tractor chassis? Be aware of any oil leaks or losses—repair them and refill the oil promptly. Avoid leaks and spills whenever you can.

Hydraulic systems are generally laid out similar to that of the engine oil—there is a dipstick to check the level, a fill-cap for adding fluid, a filter or series of filters, and a drain plug. All guidelines for checking and changing engine oil and filters apply here, as well, although the timetables for changing hydraulic fluid and filters are different.

In addition to cleaning the area around the dipstick and fill-cap, you should also take care that the hydraulic remote ports and connectors are clean and dry before inserting hoses. Inexpensive rubber caps are available to cover ports when not in use, preventing build-up of dust.

Fuel System

A good rule of thumb is that the only thing that should ever pass through the fuel system is fuel—no water, no dirt, and only cleaners that are designed to burn away with the fuel.

When working on the fuel system, avoid spilling fuel by closing the fuel flow valve if there is one, or by emptying the fuel tank. Have a can or bucket ready to catch the remaining amount of fuel in the lines once they are disconnected.

Changing fuel filters

Fuel filters come in different forms. On the smallest engines, they may just be a mesh screen at the bottom of the fuel tank. On others, they may be small inch-long plastic bodies spliced into a rubber fuel line. On vehicles and larger equipment, fuel filters are usually screw-on cartridges much like oil filters.

Water separators

On diesel engines, fuel filters will often incorporate a water-separating feature which can be drained without changing the whole filter, or there may be a free-standing water separator. In either case, these separators should be drained fairly frequently—water can choke the flow of diesel or cause significant damage if it makes it into the engine, so check weekly until you get an idea of how regularly it needs to be done. Usually it's just a matter of turning the petcock (drain valve) at the base and letting it drain until only diesel is trickling out. Many water separators are clear plastic, so that you can see the level of the water at the base.

For simple screen filters

Empty the fuel tank. Clean the screen with a clean brush in fresh fuel. Discard the fuel and replace the screen once it's clear of sediment. Clean the fuel tank, as well, if it's dirty.

For in-line fuel filters

These filters are fitted into hoses and held in place by clips. Close the fuel flow valve to minimize the fuel that will spill from the lines, or empty the fuel tank—in either case be ready with a container to catch a small amount of fuel that will be left in the lines. Remove the clips from the filter's barbs, and remove the filter. Drain any fuel remaining in the filter and discard. Replace with the new filter and open the fuel flow valve.

For screw-on cartridge filters

Close the fuel flow valve, usually located directly above or near the filter. Be ready with a container to catch the remaining fuel in the lines. Remove the old filter, drain, and discard. Lubricate the new filter's gasket with a dab of engine oil, then install the new filter and open the fuel valve.

Cleaning fuel system parts

If fuel hoses or tanks are visibly dirty or contain sediment, they should be cleaned. Some manuals will prescribe cleaning on a set timetable, as well.

To clean fuel system parts, drain all the fuel. Disassemble all parts—remove hoses, remove the tank, and so on—and use only fuel as a cleaner: gas for gas engines, diesel for diesel engines. A fresh pipe cleaner will work well on hoses, though if the hose is very long, simply running clean fuel through it may be enough. Full replacement of a fuel hose is also very cheap, if a line proves hard to clean. A clean tooth-brush or similar brush or rag will clean a fuel tank.

Priming the fuel system

Any time you introduce air into the fuel lines, it may be necessary to prime the fuel system before an engine will start—examples of such occasions are replacing fuel filters, replacing or removing fuel lines, etc. This applies also if an engine is allowed to run completely out of fuel. Some engines will prime automatically, just by cranking the engine to start. Some small engines may need some assistance using gravity to work air bubbles out of the lines. Other engines, small and large alike, will have small hand pumps to purge air bubbles. Consult your manual, if you have trouble starting the engine after a fuel system service.

Air Intake

The air for combustion must be very clean, so all combustion engines use air filters. If these filters become clogged and limit the free flow of air into the engine, the engine will start to run roughly or inefficiently. The terms air filter and air cleaner are somewhat interchangeable, though filter usually refers to a disposable item and cleaner refers to a re-usable or fixed system.

Cleaning and changing air filters

On the smallest engines, the air cleaner may be a small piece of foam or wire mesh. These air cleaners can often be rinsed or washed (according to the manual's instructions) and re-used, if they are still in good condition. These foam filters are often soaked in a light oil to help catch dust—refer to your manual for directions on oiling, if applicable.

Another type of air cleaner is a combination of foam pre-cleaner (an outer, foam wrap) on top of a cartridge-type paper-and-mesh filter element. The foam pre-cleaner is often treated as previously mentioned—cleaned or washed and sometimes oiled, sometimes just replaced. The cartridge is usually simply replaced.

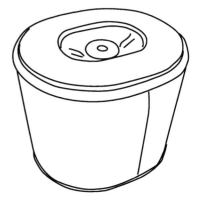

Other engines feature a simple replaceable paper element, with no pre-cleaner. Some of these paper-element filters can be cleaned by knocking them on a hard surface until they emit no more dust or by the use of an air gun (always blowing the dust from the inside toward the outside), but others must be simply replaced. If you are cleaning a filter, wear a dust mask and goggles and clean the filter away from people and equipment—large clouds of very fine dust can be discharged.

Some air cleaners feature a dust collector which uses the vortex of intake air to deposit at least some of the airborne sediment. If the dust collector is a bowl, it must be emptied and cleaned. If it is a rubber nipple mounted on the air filter housing, squeeze it open and remove any dust gathered there at the port. Check the manual for specific directions.

Some air cleaners feature an oil bath. In these cleaners, air is drawn through a wire mesh sitting in oil, and the dust is trapped by the oil. In most cases, the only service needed is to periodically change the oil and rinse the filter (usually in diesel).

Exhaust

In arid areas, small engines are required to be fitted with a spark arrestor. This device is a simple wire screen set into the engine's muffler, designed to prevent stray sparks from the engine from starting a wildfire. If you're in an arid area and have purchased equipment from a non-local distributor, it is worth checking that your equipment has a spark arrestor.

If your engine does have a spark arrestor, its screen should be cleaned weekly with a small wire brush. If your engine does not have a spark arrestor, you may need to clean the catalytic converter, also made out of wire screen. Blockages will cause heat to back up in the engine, causing damage. Check your engine's manual for specific instructions. For both spark arrestor and catalytic converter, damaged screens should be replaced.

Take care when working on the muffler, as it will be extremely hot during and after use. Let the machine cool completely in the open air before attempting to service the muffler.

Belts and Chains

Both belts and chains transmit mechanical force. An advantage to using a belt or chain, rather than a set of direct gears, is that belts and chains provide protection against overloading. So if a mechanism seizes up, its belts can slip or its chains can break—and though this might cause some peripheral damage, it is almost never as much damage as if the machine had tried to rend itself apart.

Belts and chains each have separate maintenance routines, but they both want to be tight, with slack generally taken up by **idlers**. An idler is just what it says—a rotating part designed to follow along passively, taking up slack in the belt or chain. Some idlers are spring-mounted, applying a variable and adjustable amount of force to remove slack, while others are fixed in place and require manual adjustment.

Checking belt tension and condition

The ideal belt tension is the lowest tension possible at which there is no slipping. More tension will put strain on the belt and all the bearings and pulleys. While the belt is running, there should be minimal vibration in the belt, without flapping around. V-belts at the proper tension will resist being turned over to the side more than 90 degrees. With all belts, there should be no more than minimal cracking, fraying, or *glazing* (meaning that the belt surface becomes shiny rather than dull black). Manuals will give an ideal range for *belt deflection*, the degree to which the belt can be pulled out of line.

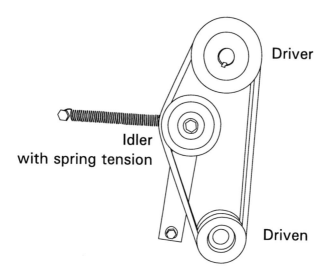

Replacing or servicing belts

Never use a pry-bar or wrench to remove or mount a belt, or else you may damage the belt in the process. Every belt-drive mechanism has a way to loosen the tension and remove its belt easily. You may need to loosen a fastener on the idler arm, allowing it to pivot freely. Sometimes when a belt is driven directly by a motor, the motor has a mounting bracket that can slide freely, once its fasteners are loosened. If a belt drive mechanism has multiple belts running parallel (that is, mounted on all the same pulleys next to each other), replace those belts together, with the identical brand and size.

Lubricating roller chain

All roller chain will rust if left exposed to the air and elements. When new chain is purchased, it comes coated in a heavy oil. WD40™ or other spray lubricants will work fine to keep chain moving smoothly, but they do not stick very well and require frequent re-application. A thicker oil will help, such as 3-in-one®. Any chains on food-handling equipment should receive only food-grade lubricants.

If a chain has seized up, it can be soaked overnight in diesel or oil to allow better penetration of the lubricant. Chains can also be replaced easily.

Repairing and splicing chains

Flat chain is simple to work with: standard tools, such as a small pry bar and a hammer, can be used for breaking and splicing flat chain. Just be sure that the chain still moves freely after the splice is made.

Roller chain is only slightly more involved. Most parts stores sell common sizes of roller chain, and more specialty chains can be ordered. Roller chain is identified by its ANSI number (*e.g.*, "number 40 roller chain") and whether it is single-strand or double-strand. There is an inexpensive tool—a **chain breaker**—which separates links by pushing out the connecting pin, allowing you to shorten a chain to however many links you need. Then by using connecting links and/or offset (aka, "odd") links you can join the two ends of your chain. Each of these link types is secured by cotter pin or spring clip.

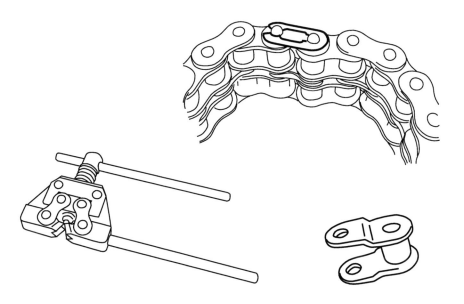

Clockwise from top: The clip of a connecting link highlighted on a double-strand roller chain; an offset link with both narrow- and wide-set plates, for making chains with odd numbers of links; chain breaker.

Adjusting Linkages

The most common linkages requiring adjustments are clutch, throttle, and brake—by changing the length of the linkage rods, you can change the action range of the controls. These linkages usually consist of rods with turnbuckles or similar adjusters. To adjust the length of a linkage rod, loosen any locking nuts and twist the turnbuckle as desired. Some linkage rods will have a threaded section with a fork end, and these rods can be adjusted by removing the pin from the fork, then turning the fork to adjust the rod length. Try out your final adjustments to make sure the linkage is set as directed, then tighten down the locking nuts to keep your setting from coming loose and wandering out of range.

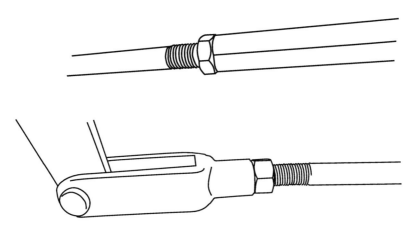

Winterization and Storage

For much of the United States, the growing season is eight to ten months, meaning that much of the farm's equipment will sit idle in storage at least for the winter. Equipment will start up much more readily, and last for more seasons, if proper care is taken in preparing it for storage.

If you are storing equipment which might contain water—an irrigation pump, or a pressure washer, for example—it should be drained completely to avoid rupture from freezing. Complex equipment such as sprayers should have non-toxic (pink) antifreeze run through them, since it is difficult to get all pockets of water out of their mechanisms.

All engines should have their coolant density tested, to make sure they have enough antifreeze for the winter ahead.

Many storage spaces lack good air flow or hold in dampness. This can cause rusting of bare metal—everything from mower blades to cylinder sleeves to control cables and so on. Most manuals will instruct you to lightly oil exposed parts such as cables and mower blades, but refer to your manual for detailed instructions.

Tractor/vehicle batteries will work better during the winter if fully-charged and stored in a warm (but well-ventilated) space.

Most manuals will recommend a full cleaning, lubrication, and filter change before the winter. In addition, it is usually recommended to empty all fuel tanks and fuel lines, so that equipment is ready to accept fresh fuel in the spring. Running an engine on fuel with the right amount of fuel preservative for a few minutes is an acceptable alternative—let it burn through enough of the old fuel that you can be sure only the preserved fuel is left in the system.

Lastly, and this applies to storage at any time of year, protect your machinery from rodents and insects. Animals will climb into and nest in just about any opening, so keep fuel tanks, fuel lines, crankcases, and so on, all shut up. This especially applies year-round to irrigation equipment, whose pipe fittings are usually just the right size for a nest.

Troubleshooting Startup Problems

Two- and Four-stroke engines with pull-start

What's the ambient temperature? Some engines, old and worn-out or otherwise, do not like starting in the cold. Every engine starts better on a warm day. If you have persistent problems with an engine not starting in the cold, keep it indoors in a warm place. Often, while a low ambient temperature can seem to be the root of the problem, the temperature really only exacerbates a more fundamental problem with the engine.

How old is the fuel? If the fuel in the tank has been sitting in disuse for more than a few weeks without having had fuel preservative added, it may lack the vigor to burn readily. If this is the case, drain the fuel from the tank and lines. Replace it with fresh gas (or gas and oil mix for two-strokes), with the right amount of preservative added. You can sometimes run on old gas, but it will feel like beating your head against a wall while you try to start the engine. One solution can be to spray starter fluid into the carburetor, as directed—this can sometimes be enough to get the engine going, and a warmer engine will deal better with the poor gas. The gas should still be replaced as soon as possible, as poor combustion will only dirty the engine's workings further. **Note that starter fluid is not for use in diesel engines.**

Is the engine flooded? The term *flooding an engine* refers to a condition where the combustion chamber is too full of fuel, and the spark plug, being wet with fuel, cannot ignite it. Most small engines have a choke—if the start cord has been pulled repeatedly with the choke on, more and more gas has been poured into the combustion chamber without burning off. Thus, after a certain point, just pulling the cord will actually make the engine less likely to start. Remove the spark plug and inspect it—is the plug wet with gas? Turn off the choke and throttle up, if it is. This will let the maximum amount of air run through the engine, so pull the cord a handful of times to clear the extra fuel out of the cylinder. Return the spark plug to the engine, but be sure to start threading it by hand before using a wrench. Tighten until flush, do not overtighten.

What's the condition of the spark plug? Remove the spark plug and inspect it. If the plug is covered in carbon build-up from incomplete combustion, it may not be able to spark readily. You can clean the plug with a light wire brush or rag if you're in a rush and don't have a spare plug, but really it's worth replacing the spark plug. Note the brand and code on the plug, as this will help you find a replacement.

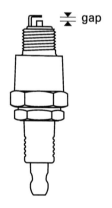

If the spark plug is clean, you should still check the gap against the manual's recommendation. New plugs must also be gapped before installation. To do this, look up the proper gap in the engine's manual. Then, take a **spark plug gap gauge** and insert it between the electrodes. Bend the outer (lateral) electrode to make the gap exactly fit the correct gauge.

Is the fuel system clean? Is there sediment in the fuel tank or fuel

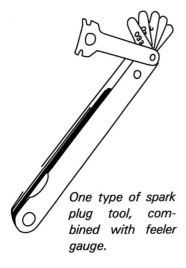

One type of spark plug tool, combined with feeler gauge.

lines? Is there build-up? If so, it will have to be cleaned out. Do not use water or any water-based cleaner. Gasoline is just about the only cleaner you should use on a gas engine's fuel system. Pour out the old, dirty gas into a container reserved for waste gas. Use clean brushes, pipe cleaners, or rags to clean out the fuel lines and tank.

Is the air filter dirty or clogged? Is the carburetor dirty? The air filter is easy—simply clean or replace as instructed by your manual. Carburetors are a common cause of rough start-up or running, and they can be lightly cleaned using spray cans from an auto parts store. A thorough cleaning of a gunky carburetor requires some disassembly, though. If you're up for it, look up more detailed instructions. If not, take it to a repair shop.

Are the electrical connections clean and working? Corroded terminals and worn-out switches of all kinds are common on farm equipment. If all else fails, check these parts. Dirty electrical terminals should be cleaned with a wire brush: anything from dull oxidation to white or blue powder is corrosion. Wires should have good insulation on them to prevent short-circuiting, so battered wires should be replaced. Jiggling a switch might help determine if its contacts are intermittent.

If you think you have a good spark plug, you can remove it from the engine but keep it attached to its wire. Then ground the outer (lateral) electrode against a metal surface on the engine. Pull the start cord—if you cannot see a spark, there is no power reaching the plug. You may have a bad connection.

Four-stroke engine with battery ignition

Almost all the same advice applies as above, though any startup trouble is much more likely to be electrical at its root. If the engine has a battery-powered starter, **avoid engaging the ignition for more than 10 seconds at a time.** After 10 seconds, turn the key off and let the battery rest for 30 seconds. Continuously turning over the engine will wear out the starter and battery. Also, never bypass the regular starter wiring. If a safety switch has failed and prevents tractor start, have it fixed immediately. Waiting any amount of time creates opportunity for serious injury from starting in gear.

Does the engine try to turn over, but only weakly? Or do you get a clicking noise when you try to start? This weakness or clicking indicates either a weak battery or a poor connection. Either way, not enough voltage is reaching the starter. You should first check that the battery terminals are clean and free of corrosion, and that the battery cables are free of corrosion on their contact surface. Best for this operation is a battery terminal brush. Reseat the battery cables tightly on their terminals and try again. You can try jumping the engine from another vehicle with the same size of battery if that doesn't work, as it's possible that the battery, with a bad connection, was not able to charge while the vehicle was last running. If you still get clicking or weak turnover while jumping, check the connections at the other end of the battery cables—to the ground (chassis) and to the starter. These connections also occasionally need to be cleaned and re-seated. Sometimes you may get good power (12+ V) at the starter, but the engine still will not start. This may indicate a bad starter motor.

Are other electrical connections clean and working? Over time electrical safety switches can wear out, so if your equipment has a safety switch—most commonly one which prevents starting while in gear or while the PTO is engaged—you may need to jiggle the affected controls a bit to make or break contact, as needed. So even though you might not be in gear, and the PTO might be off, the safety switch thinks you're in gear or the PTO is on and is thus preventing you from starting.

If the electrical system is equipped with fuses, check that the fuses are intact and not burned-out.

In addition, corroded terminals and worn-out switches of all kinds are common on farm equipment. If all else fails, check these parts. Electrical terminals should be cleaned with a wire brush and put back together. Wires should have good insulation on them to prevent short-circuiting. If you understand the wiring on your engine, an electrical circuit tester can help pinpoint problems.

Jump-starting an Engine

If you need to jump start an engine, there are first a few items to check. Turn off both ignitions and any electrical accessories, with both transmissions in park or neutral with the brake on. Make sure the two batteries have matching voltage ratings. Also make sure the vehicles are not touching. If the battery to be jumped is sealed and maintenance free, you're ready to go; otherwise remove the vent caps and lay a damp cloth over the holes. Do not smoke or hold an open flame near batteries. Safety glasses are recommended, in case of battery explosion.

Connect the jumper cables in the order shown below. Take care not to let clamps accidentally touch each other.

DEAD BATTERY

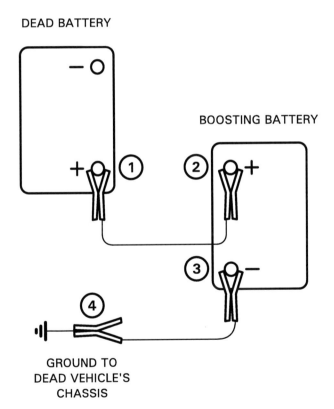

BOOSTING BATTERY

GROUND TO
DEAD VEHICLE'S
CHASSIS

1. Clamp one end of the red cable to the + (positive) terminal on the dead battery.

2. Clamp the other end of the red cable to the + (positive) terminal on the boosting battery.

3. Clamp one end of the black cable to the − (negative) terminal on the boosting battery.

4. Clamp the remaining end of the black cable to a good ground on the dead vehicle—this should be the metal chassis or frame, but not the − (negative) terminal of the battery.*

Start the engine of the good battery, then start the engine of the dead battery. If the engine cranks for 10 seconds but doesn't start, let the battery rest for 30 seconds before trying again. Also double check that the battery is the problem and not something else. If the engine won't crank at all, you may have loose connections in your jumping setup or a bad ground. It may also be that the battery is not the source of the problem.

Disconnect the clamps in the reverse order—4, 3, 2, 1. Let the engine that was jump-started run for at least half an hour without stopping, if possible. If all the connections are good, the alternator is working, and the battery is able to hold a charge, then half an hour of running should give enough juice to let the engine start on its own next time.

However, a good alternative to letting the engine run (and using fuel) is to use a plug-in battery charger.

* It is common practice on farms to disregard this last direction and clamp right to the battery's terminal. Most of the time, this is fine on a maintenance-free battery. However, the reason for all the warnings is that a spark from the cable to the battery terminal might ignite hydrogen gas from the battery, resulting in an explosion. Each year in the U.S., hundreds of people get serious chemical burns from this hazard, so try to find a good bare-metal spot on the chassis to clamp that negative cable.

General-use Field Equipment

This section describes a basic assortment of small equipment for the farm. I include these items in this volume because they are fairly universal in their distribution and general in their use—they are tools for ongoing tasks such as light field work, grounds maintenance, irrigation, and transportation. This section is in no way exhaustive, and there will be other equipment you'll need to use on the farm. However, this is a good place to start, an introduction to concepts that can be applied to power equipment in general.

I avoid discussing chainsaws here, since chainsaws are not a tool for casual discussion. There is a lot of detailed information about safe operation and proper maintenance of chainsaws, best conveyed by the manufacturer's manual. So if you are going to use a chainsaw, read the manual and, if possible, attend a workshop on safe operation and maintenance. It's not as simple as adding bar and chain oil every time.

I also avoid discussing generators here. If you rely heavily on electricity to keep your operation going—for example, if you rely on a well for your water—I recommend you speak with an electrician regarding generator options. An incorrectly sized generator can be a hazard to your electrical appliances, and a poorly-installed generator can be a hazard for the linesmen working to restore power at the grid.

For each of the items, as much as it's appropriate, I include a general description of its workings, common maintenance tasks, and troubleshooting.

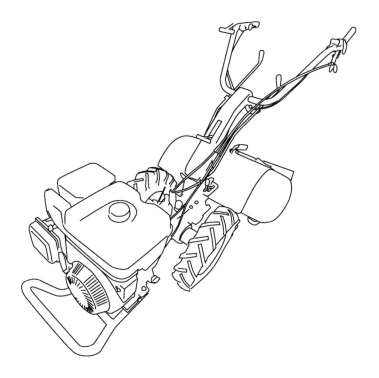

Walk-Behind Tractor

These tractors have been around since the beginning of powered farm equipment, and they are still common throughout world agriculture. Today they are more common elsewhere than in the United States, where they are often equated with the simple rototiller (which, though very similar, cannot accept a diversity of implements). These machines are also known as two-wheel tractors or single-axle tractors. The makes most popular in the U.S. today are European—BCS and Grillo, mostly—although Asian manufacturers also offer a number of models. Gravely is an American manufacturer of walk-behind tractors, and though their tiller attachments are no longer in production, older models with tiller heads are occasionally available.

For the smaller farm, these tractors can be just the right scale, speeding the process of bed preparation significantly. For the larger farm, these tractors can still hold great utility—getting into high tunnels and greenhouses, cultivating pathways between well-established plants, and so on. The larger units can offer significant advantages in power over the smaller units, and some even have diesel engines.

Although the upper-end brand-name models can seem quite expensive, they offer real benefits. Established manufacturers will offer service and support through their dealerships, with better long-term availability of replacement parts. Commercial models will stand up better to heavy use and offer features like differential drive, making tight turns possible.

These tractors usually have transmissions with a full range of gears as well as a separate control for engaging and disengaging the PTO. The control linkages and levers can become very sticky and difficult to operate over time, but regular lubrication will be rewarded with easier and safer operation.

The most common attachment is a rototiller, available in various widths for different applications. There are other tillage implements less common, as well as rotary and flair mowers, snow blowers, etc. They are also able to pull specialized wagons and carts.

Safety is a serious concern with walk-behind tractors, compared with the typical four-wheel variety. With walk-behind tractors the operator must exercise extra care not to put a foot into the implement workings; the operator of a four-wheel tractor, on the other hand, is at least further removed from a mower's blades or tiller's tines, and often shielded by the tractor chassis. A walk-behind tractor in poor working condition can also be very difficult to steer, control, or stop effectively, especially if the operator is slight or lacks physical strength. All current models have a safety-stop switch that, when released, cuts off the engine. If you are losing control of the tractor, let go of the switch and let the tractor cut off. Read all the advice from the manufacturer on safety precautions.

There are various reasons to consider walk-behind tractors for your farm, but there are good reasons to consider alternatives, as well. In the United States, there are many older four-wheel tractors which are readily available, often in good condition, for not much more money than a new walk-behind. In the U.S., implements and parts for four-wheel tractors are often easier to find and more versatile. Four-wheel tractors are often many times faster in accomplishing tasks, and in some ways are easier to operate. All of these factors must be considered when deciding what equipment is appropriate for your farm.

Common maintenance routine

Engines on walk-behind tractors are typically four-stroke gas engines (sometimes diesel) in the 6-15 Horsepower range. See the chapter on four-stroke engine maintenance for engine care and troubleshooting.

Lubrication. Follow the manual's recommendations for joints and bearings that need regular lubrication or oil-level checks. This usually includes all hinges and joints on control levers and linkages, which need regular oil to move smoothly and without hassle. The manual will also recommend lubricating or checking any implements' moving parts.

Regular cleaning. Keep dirt or field trash from caking up on the tractor's parts by cleaning it with a water hose or air gun after use. Avoid getting water on a hot engine or into the engine's ports, or into jackets around control cables, or any other rust-prone location.

Replacing tiller tines. All roto-tillers eventually need their tines replaced, as they get worn down from abrasion by the soil. Check several times a season that your tiller's tines are still fully formed and able to perform their duties. Replacement is simple, a matter of nuts and bolts, but care should be taken to re-mount them in the same orientation as before—so that the sharpened blade enters the soil first.

Sharpening mower blades. If you use a mower—whether rotary, flail, or sickle-bar type—the blades must be kept sharpened and balanced. This is accomplished with careful use of a grinder, and the blades usually need to be removed from the implement before sharpening. For rotary and flail mowers to run smoothly without excessive vibration, the weight of opposing blades must be balanced. If you remove material from one blade with aggressive sharpening, you may need to remove a similar amount from the other blade. Bent or worn-down blades should be replaced.

Winterization. Most manuals have a checklist of maintenance tasks to accomplish before storage. Beyond engine maintenance, these tasks will be mostly lubrication for walk-behind tractors, for all the linkages and bearings most likely to corrode or seize up over the winter. If you have sprayer or water pump implements for your tractor, those will have to be drained, or else run-through with non-toxic (pink) antifreeze.

Troubleshooting

Tractor requires excessive downward pressure while tilling. The soil being tilled might be very compacted, especially if you're trying to break sod. Try tilling in a lower gear with high throttle. If you're breaking sod, manufacturers recommend tilling once at a shallow depth, followed by a second pass at the desired depth of tillage.

You might also confirm that the tines on the tiller are installed in the proper direction, such that the sharp end of the tines enters the soil first. If the tines are full of field trash, that should also be removed before tilling.

Tractor has no traction in soft soil and requires excessive force to steer. The simplest solution, if your tractor is so equipped, is to lock the differential. Not all walk-behinds have a differential drive, but the ones that do feature an option to the lock the wheels in step with each other, preventing spin-out and loss of traction. Just be sure to unlock the differential when you need to turn around at the end of the row.

A further solution is to add wheel weights, which are available from your dealer. Mounted onto the tire rims, the weights will help the tires dig into the soil more and increase the effectiveness of their tread. Make sure that you're using the deep-tread field tires, also, and not the shallow-tread lawn tires.

Tractor is difficult to handle even when not tilling. Some models are better balanced than others. One recommendation is to use the parts provided by the manufacturer for aiding in transport: wheels to hold up the tiller in transport, and a sulky (trailing seat) to ride when not tilling.

There are also extensions available for the mounting brackets of implements. These parts allow for shifting the center of gravity of the tractor-and-implement, if that will help in achieving a better overall balance and ease-of-operation.

Also check that, if your tractor has a differential drive, it is not locked or seized. If your tractor lacks a differential drive, you might consider a model equipped with one, as these models can be somewhat easier to turn.

I would recommend considering all of the above options, as well as conferring with your dealer, before concluding that you simply lack the strength or size to handle the tiller.

Clutch is frozen in the engaged position. Some models have cone clutches which have a tendency to seize up when parked. If you cannot squeeze the clutch control handle, the clutch itself may be rusted. A simple preventative solution is to park the tractor with the clutch disengaged—that is, with the handle locked in the squeezed position. This way, all parts are kept separate in storage and unable to fuse. It's all the more important, though, to park the tractor on a level surface with blocks around the wheels, as it will be able to roll freely.

The solution to a thoroughly-frozen clutch is to disassemble it—which involves removing the engine—and free it up with lubricant. Consult with your service center, as they can walk you through the process.

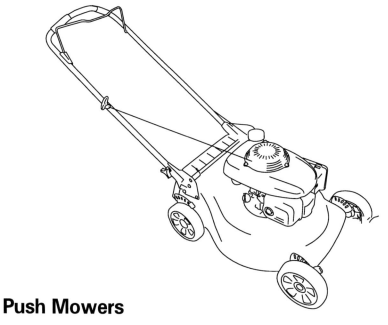

Push Mowers

Push mowers generally have four-stroke gas engines, although electric models for home-owners are becoming widely available. Mowers are used for tasks like pathway maintenance—ideally when a cover crop has been sown between beds—and general grounds maintenance.

Many push-mowers are now self-propelled, which can greatly ease the burden of operating them for long periods. All the same, most push-mowers are designed for home use on lawns, that is, even ground with relatively short grass. Farm fields often feature much rougher terrain and taller plant matter than mowers like to work with. Repeatedly running over obstacles or mowing into dirt will mangle your mower's blade. Also be aware that mowers will not safely clear any irrigation hoses or tubing left across a pathway.

Be careful never to tip gas mowers with the air filter pointing downward, nor to tip mowers more than 90 degrees in any other direction. Fuel can easily flow through the carburetor and saturate the air filter, making the mower impossible to start until the fuel evaporates. One solution is to drain all fuel from the tank before turning over the mower.

With all mowers, make sure safety guards are in place and operational. Avoid running over brush or gravel or debris, which can be hurtled out of the mower and cause injury. Wear ear protection and a dusk mask.

Common maintenance routine

See the chapter on regular maintenance for engine care and troubleshooting.

Safety check. Make sure all nuts and bolts and screws are tight. Also make sure that all guards are in place and undamaged—these plastic parts are unfortunately easy to break, but also easy and cheap to replace. They are important for the safety of the operator and others.

Regular cleaning. Keep the mower deck (top surface of the mower housing) and the engine area free of debris and dust. Rain-soaked clippings hold their moisture and lead to rust. Debris on and around the engine can lead to engine overheating or clog the air filter. The air filter itself should be checked every time the mower is used and knocked free of dust and debris. The underside of the mower should also be cleaned regularly to prevent buildup of clippings—drain the gas and disconnect the spark plug before tipping the mower (with air filter facing up). Just scrape the clippings away, and avoid using water.

Lubrication. Lubricate the blades as directed (or if directed) by your manual. Give a shot of a light lubricant to all the control levers and cables. Also lubricate the wheels and their height adjusters, as well as any guard flaps or doors which hinge open and closed.

Belt tensioning and replacement. If your mower blades are driven by a belt from the engine, follow your manual's guidelines for checking the belt and replacing it.

Sharpen or replace blades. The blades must be kept sharpened and balanced. This is usually performed once or twice a season with careful use of a grinder. The blades usually need to be removed from the implement before sharpening. For rotary mowers to run smoothly without excessive vibration, the weight of opposing blades must be balanced. If you remove material from one blade from aggressive sharpening, or if one blade is damaged by hitting an obstruction, you may need to remove a similar amount from the other blade. Bent or worn-down blades should be replaced. This task is easily and affordably accomplished by a small engine shop.

Winterization. Clean off all clippings from above and below. Drain the gas, or run gas with preservative through the engine for a couple minutes. Lubricate all controls, levers, doors, wheels, and blade bearings with a light oil or silicone spray. Apply oil or a light grease to the blades to prevent them from rusting. Keep mower out of the weather.

Troubleshooting

Mower has electric starter; motor will not turn over. If the mower has a battery, it also has a fuse. Check that the fuse is not burned out, and replace if necessary. Also check that there is no safety feature preventing the mower from starting (is the mower in drive?). Otherwise, refer to the section on troubleshooting startup problems for four-stroke engines with battery ignition.

Mower is hard to push while mowing. Mowers designed for lawns don't like uneven ground or especially tall grass. Try adjusting the wheel height and raising the throttle. Also check that the mower is not clogged and that the blades are rust-free and sharp.

Mower vibrates excessively. The blades may be damaged and in need of a balancing. Follow your manual's recommendations or take the mower to a shop.

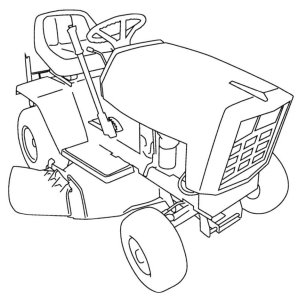

Riding Mowers and Garden Tractors

Riding mowers are also designed for the lawn environment. Beyond their lawn-mowing capacity, they can sometimes be useful, insofar as they have some other implements available as attachments, such as tillers or dozer blades. For that reason, some models have front hitches, rear hitches, or rear PTOs. Some models have geared transmissions, while others use a hydrostatic drive.

Unfortunately, most of these mowers have a relatively low clearance and lawn-tread tires, so they are prone to getting stuck around a farm. They are also relatively slow and noisy. If you're looking for a vehicle to pull a wagon or cart on rough terrain, you might instead consider an ATV or an old pickup truck or tractor.

If you need to work on the blades or any other part of the mowing deck's underside, you may need to detach the mowing deck from the mower. Check the manual for instructions.

Common maintenance routine

See the chapter on regular maintenance for engine care and troubleshooting.

Safety check. Make sure all nuts and bolts and screws are tight. Also make sure that all guards are in place and undamaged—these plastic parts are unfortunately easy to break, but also easy and cheap to replace. They are important for the safety of the operator and others. Check that the emergency cut-off works by trying it out—engage it while the engine and mower are running and make sure the engine stops as it should. Check that the seat cut-off works—if the engine is running and you stand up, the engine should cut off. Check that the parking brake prevents the tractor from moving. If the steering is finicky—turning to one side faster than the other—then adjust the drag links on the steering linkage to be even.

Regular cleaning. Keep the mower deck (top surface of the mower housing) free of debris and dust. Rain-soaked clippings hold their moisture and lead to rust. Clean the front grille and all inside the hood, as debris on and around the engine's cooling fins can lead to engine overheating. The air filter itself should be checked and knocked free of dust and debris—re-oil the pre-cleaner if necessary, per the manual's instructions. Clean the battery terminals if they're corroded, and coat them in petroleum jelly. The underside of the mower should also be cleaned to prevent buildup of clippings—some mowers have garden hose hookups on the mower deck to simplify this task.

Lubrication. Lubricate the blades as directed (or if directed) by your manual. Give a shot of a light lubricant to all the control levers and cables, all pedals' pivot points, and the steering linkage and the axles. Also lubricate the mower's wheels and the deck's wheels.

Belt tensioning and replacement. If your mower blades are driven by a belt from the PTO, follow your manual's guidelines for checking the belt and replacing it.

Sharpen or replace blades. The blades must be kept sharpened and balanced. This is usually performed once or twice a season with careful use of a grinder. The blades usually need to be removed from the implement before sharpening. For rotary mowers to run smoothly without excessive vibration, the weight of opposing blades must be balanced. If you remove material from one blade from aggressive sharpening, or if one blade is damaged by hitting an obstruction, you may need to remove a similar amount from the other blade. Bent or worn-down blades should be replaced. This task is easily and affordably accomplished by a small engine shop.

Level the mowing deck. Park on a level surface and check the level of the mowing deck relative to the ground, front-to-back and side-to-side. Use the adjusting bolts or pins to make corrections. Most mowers want a specified incline from front-to-back (see the manual) but perfect level side-to-side.

Winterization. Clean off all clippings from above and below. Drain the gas, or run gas with preservative through the engine for a couple minutes. Lubricate all controls, levers, doors, wheels, and blade bearings with a light oil or silicone spray. Apply oil or a light grease to the blades to prevent them from rusting. Keep mower out of the weather.

Troubleshooting

Motor will not turn over. If the mower has a battery, it also has a fuse. Check that the fuse is not burned out, and replace if necessary. Also check that there is no safety feature (Is the PTO on? Is the parking brake not engaged?) preventing the mower from starting. Otherwise, refer to the section on troubleshooting startup for four-stroke engines with battery ignition.

Engine overheats. Check engine oil level and top up with the appropriate grade oil if necessary. Clear away debris from the hood's louvers and from the air intake and cooling fins on the engine.

Mower has trouble cutting grass. Mowers designed for lawns don't like uneven ground or especially tall grass. Try adjusting the cutting height and raising the throttle. Alternatively, try moving at a slower groundspeed with high throttle to keep the blades moving quickly, or try cutting a narrower swath. Make sure the blades are sharp, straight, and rust-free.

Mower fails to cut grass evenly. Check that the mower is not clogged and that the blades are rust-free and sharp. Check that the deck's level, and check that tire pressure is equal among all four tires.

Mower vibrates excessively. The blades may be loose, or damaged and in need of a balancing. Tighten bolts and screws. Follow your manual's recommendations for balancing the blades or take the mower to a shop.

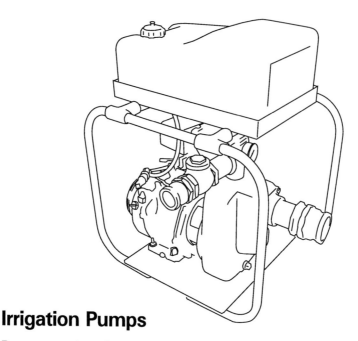

Irrigation Pumps

Pumps consist of two main parts: the pump impeller (which pushes the water), and the motor which drives the impeller. Small irrigation pumps can be gas or diesel, electric, or PTO-driven. Electric and PTO-driven pumps will seem to require less time troubleshooting—mostly because electric motors are wonderfully low-maintenance, and PTO-driven pumps are as reliable as the tractors which drive them. All the same, the advice here is still worth reading: there are plenty of subtleties to the workings of pumps beyond the motors which drive them.

For gas- and diesel-powered small pumps, the motor usually takes half or more of all the maintenance time. Part of this is due to the nature of pumps—they sit off on river banks, away from the shop and out of view, mostly stationary, where farm personnel rarely go except to start the pumps, not to maintain them. Strategies must be developed, then, to make it easier and more convenient to service the pump. For this reason, keeping engine oil and a grease gun (if appropriate to your pump) near the pump station or in an irrigation vehicle will make maintenance much more likely to happen.

> Be aware that if you are going to keep engine oil, fuel, or grease out in the field, it's required to be sealed from the elements and prevented from dripping or spilling onto the

ground or into water. A tightly sealed plastic container, lashed in place above the flood line, will do the job. An alternative is sending out your irrigation operator with a designated tool bag containing all the items he or she might need.

Take advantage of rainy periods when irrigation is less in-demand and bring your pumps in for service. Pumps are often forced to do without regular maintenance during the season because of the inconvenience of fetching the pumps back to the farm. Anything you can do to make it easier to transport pumps, then, will make good maintenance more likely to happen. Mount pumps on a trailer, or mount wheels onto the pump's frame; keep a suction hose and other appropriate fittings at each pump station, so that they don't need to be moved as often as the pumps; build better vehicle access to pump stations; use an all-terrain dolly or your tractor's hydraulic loader to carry small pumps with less effort; make fuel tanks easily detachable with quick-disconnect fuel lines. Beyond the problem of transport, the sum total of regular maintenance activities only takes about half an hour on small pumps, so it's not out-of-the-question even during busy periods.

The impeller is the business end of the pump. In most small irrigation pumps, the impeller works by centrifugal force—a rotating disk flings the water out from the center and on out of the pump housing. The impeller is water-cooled, so a pump that has run dry or lost prime and runs too long without any water in the housing will overheat and damage itself.

Pumps pull water up from their source through a suction hose. A suction hose requires a very tight seal at all seams to function properly. Also, for the quality of the water that is pumped, the suction hose strainer end must be away from the stream/pond bed and still far enough below the surface to avoid sucking in air. For this reason, the strainer end is often fitted with a combination of weights and floats.

Priming a pump means filling the suction hose with water, all the way up to meet the impeller. A pump must be primed in order to push water. Some pumps are self-priming, including most small pumps. This means that, if they are started with their housing full of water already, they will be able to create enough suction in an empty, air-filled suc-

76

Situating a suction hose and strainer.

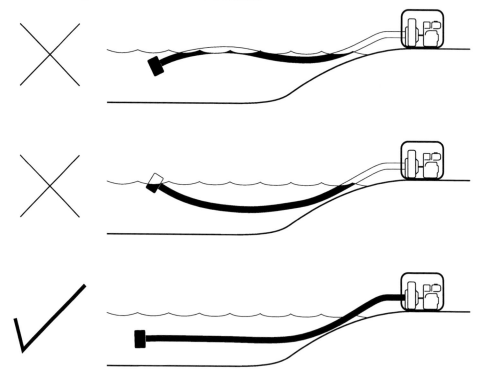

tion hose to eventually draw the water up to the impeller and start pumping. Self-priming pumps usually need high throttle to prime themselves, but they should be throttled down once they start pushing water—too much pressure while filling the lines can break fittings (the water hammer* effect). Other pumps need to be primed manually, usually by a hand-operated primer pump. In either case, water can only be drawn up a certain height by suction. Even before that physical limit, there is a practical limit where a pump will have difficulty priming or maintaining prime. Place pumps as close as is reasonable to water level while still maintaining solid, level footing.

Water hammer refers to the pressure wave as water (or any fluid) fills pipes and pushes out air, or abruptly stops or changes direction. A common example is the shudder that can come from suddenly closing a household spigot. Farmers must be aware of the effect and avoid closing irrigation valves suddenly or filling irrigation lines too quickly. The force of the water can blow out drip fittings, dislodge pipes from each other, or split hoses and clamps.

If your water source is prone to rapid fluctuations in water level, be alert and ready to fetch your pump at any time. Keep fuel cans secured far away from any potential flood level. Tie ropes, straps, or chains from your pump and suction hose to sturdy trees as insurance against losing equipment to sudden flooding or a deteriorating stream bank.

Some pumps come equipped with protective circuits designed to shut off the pump in event of a problem. The primary anticipated problem is a blowout in the water line, resulting in a rapid pressure loss as the water floods the area around the rupture. The circuit operates as a pressure-sensitive switch, then—if line pressure goes down, it will cut off the pump. These switches, when working properly, need to be reset before each irrigation. Some pumps have sensors on their oil level or engine temperature, but if you do not see explicit mention of a protective circuit in the manual, you might assume that your pump has none. Whether you have protective circuits or not, your maintenance routine should be the same, since you should never rely on the switches alone to protect your equipment—it has been my experience that on the farm they do not often function as intended. Valuable as these circuits are, they are one of the first things to check in event of difficulty operating a pump.

Common maintenance routine

See the chapter on regular maintenance for engine care and troubleshooting.

Self-priming pump: make sure housing is full of water. If unsure, take off the outlet hose and pour a couple gallons of water in. You may need to tilt the pump back a bit while pouring.

Lubricate any grease points. Commonly the check valve handle and the impeller shaft have grease zerks, though smaller pumps may be self-lubricating. If using a PTO-driven pump, check oil in gearbox; lubricate PTO-shaft and universal joints.

Check the packing gland. If pump's packing gland is designed to be water lubricated, make sure it's dripping the right amount. (Check with your dealer as to whether this applies to your pump.)

Situate suction hose at proper level in water. It's easy to improvise floats and sinks to keep the strainer above the river or pond bottom and below the surface—a combination of old plastic bottles and cinder blocks will do. Just make sure everything is well-secured, to avoid littering.

Refuel very carefully, making sure not to get sand or dust into the tank. Clean the fuel can's spout and the area around the fuel cap before filling.

Winterization. Lube all appropriate parts, change oil. Add fuel with fuel preservative, and run the pump to clear out any old fuel from the lines. Then empty the tank and close the breather valve on fuel tank, if appropriate, to prevent contamination from dust or water. If the gas tank has sediment in it, now is a good time to clean it out. Most important: drain the impeller housing, by tipping the pump down as much as possible and opening drain plugs.

Troubleshooting

Pump won't start or quits during operation. Check engine oil. Check that pump is perfectly level in place, as many small engines have oil sensors which will prevent operation if oil becomes low. Sensors can be fooled into detecting low oil if the engine is on a tilt. These sensors can also wear out or become dirty, so they may eventually need to be replaced or cleaned. If your pump has an electronic pressure switch, be sure to reset it before trying to start the pump, or even hold down the reset button while starting the pump. If the gas tank has a breather valve and/or a flow valve, make sure these are open.

Otherwise, check the regular maintenance section on startup troubleshooting for the appropriate engine type.

Water lines won't pressurize. Check that the pump is fully primed. Check that the right lines are open or closed, and that water is not freely flowing out of an opening or break in the line. Check that your pump is capable of the flow rate necessary to pressurize all open lines—this may require taking into account pressure loss from height or from friction within the hose or pipe. Pressure drops very quickly when pushed up a rise, or when a large amount of water is pushed through small hoses. Your irrigation dealer has charts to calculate these amounts.

Pump won't prime. This is a very common problem and source of many headaches. Think through the steps of targeting the problem:

If the pump is self-priming, is the housing full of water? Pour more water in the outlet until it overflows. Give the pump full throttle while it primes itself—then throttle back once it starts pushing water.

Check the suction hose—does it have any air bubbles caught in it? Suction hoses work best when there are no humps, just one steady rise from strainer up to the pump. Humps can trap air bubbles and cause persistent loss of prime.

How does the suction hose fit to the pump? Does it have a good seal at the gasket? Are gravity and the weight of the water-filled hose pulling too hard at the seal, letting a small amount of air in? A solution to this problem can often be jury-rigged by propping up the hose to take the weight off of the joint at the impeller. However, a better solution might just entail re-seating the suction hose in another orientation on the gasket, or applying mineral oil to the gasket. There are also a variety of different suction hose fittings, **ball-type** being the fitting with the most consistent, positive seal.

Aluminum or poly quick-couplers are usually sufficient for smaller (less than 4") suction hoses.

If the pump is manually-primed, the hose is full of water, and yet the pump won't start pushing, try working the priming pump while the pump itself is running. This co-operation between primer and impeller can produce the extra little pull a pump needs to prime. Raising the pump throttle may also help.

Above: Locking quick-couplers. Below: Ball-type coupler on a large suction hose.

Mechanical seals and packing glands form the seal around the driveshaft where it enters the pump housing, and they can also be a source of priming problems. Talk to your dealer on this topic.

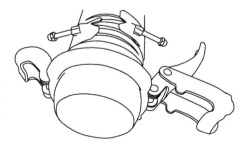

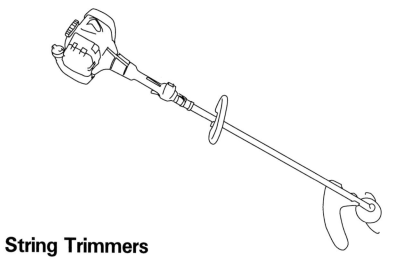

String Trimmers

Also called weed whackers or weed eaters, these machines are available with electric motors, but electric models generally require access to a power supply and are thus not very portable. Two-stroke gas engines are more common for farm and landscape applications. Sawblade or winged heads are available as brush-clearing alternatives to the typical string head, although these other heads do not kick away debris as well as string does. These other heads are also more of a hazard than string, if they should strike the operator or an obstruction.

The primary safety hazard with string trimmers is ricochets: the string can easily fling pebbles or other debris in the direction of the operator or of others nearby. Take care when starting the trimmer that the area is free of debris. Eye and ear protection are necessary. Also take care not to strain your back or neck with repetitive swinging motions. Use a comfortable support strap, or take the time to make the strap comfortable.

Note that most trimmer heads thread onto their mounting shaft with reverse thread. That is, right is loosen and left is tighten.

Common maintenance routine

See the chapter on regular maintenance for engine care and troubleshooting.

Safety check. Make sure the trimmer guard is properly and securely placed to protect the operator from flinging debris. Check that the engine-stop switch moves freely and functions as intended. Check that the trimming attachment is stopped when the engine is idling, and adjust as needed. Make sure the trimmer head is tightly screwed onto its shaft and undamaged. Check that the vibration damping parts are all in good shape and working. Make sure there are no fuel leaks, and check all bolts and screws for tightness.

Cord winding. Be sure to use cordage that's properly sized for your trimmer head. The manual will help with this choice, but it's easy to tell when string is too big and has difficulty feeding through the grommets on the side of the trimmer head. Take time to read the manual's instructions for winding the string—poorly-wound string will not feed correctly and may cause imbalances and vibration. Also check that the trimmer guard's cutter is functioning—its role is to keep the working cord length equal between the two strands.

Regular cleaning. Clean the outside of the machine, starting at the guard and trimmer head—remove anything wound up on the trimmer to prevent it from getting into the bearing. Clean the outside of the motor, making sure that cool, clean air can get into the housing. Clean the air filter and oil it as instructed, and make sure the filter guard is unblocked. Clean debris away from the engine's cooling fins—usually on the flywheel and on the engine block. Clean the outside of the carburetor, as well as the spark arrestor, if your trimmer has one. Check that the fuel filter and lines are clean and free from sediment. Clean the spark plug if it has carbon build-up. Some manuals suggest replacing the plug as often as monthly.

Lubrication. Use only two-stroke fuel mix in two-stroke engines, and only according to the manufacturer's ratio. Most trimmers have a bevel gear down at the trimmer head. These rarely need additional grease, but it's good to check every now and then. Follow manufacturers' recommendations for grease type.

Troubleshooting

Check the chapter on regular maintenance for troubleshooting engine problems.

String will not feed out or gets lost in housing. First check that you have fed the string onto the spool exactly as directed. Second check that the grommets through which the string exits the housing are in their proper place and the string moves freely through them. Lastly, check that the housing and the feed mechanism have not been gummed up by banging too forcefully against the ground—gentle bumps against the ground, while giving moderate throttle, are all that are usually called for. With a little plastic-safe lubricant or fine sandpaper (to remove burrs), you can often make the spool and release-button slide around more easily.

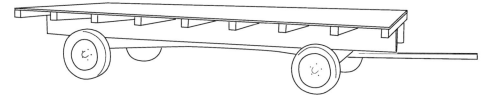

Carts and Wagons

Trailers are one of the simple conveniences which make farm work significantly easier. Combined with a conveyor belt, they can become an integral part of a harvest routine. They require little maintenance, but keeping your wagons in good order will ensure they'll be there when you need them.

Never rely on workers to hold down an unwieldy load on a wagon or truck bed. If a load is unsecured, it is a danger to the people on the wagon. The best practice is to use ratchet straps, available in all lengths and load ratings. It is very simple to install mounting hardware so that a wagon load may be secured with straps—just make sure that the wood or metal into which the hardware mounts is sturdy and solid. Well cared-for straps will last for years.

Common maintenance routine

Safety check. The trailer deck should be kept in good shape. Keep it free of dirt and debris and it will stand up better to the weather. Repair broken planks or stringers. Add anti-slip tape if the deck gets too slick when wet. Check that the hitch is in good condition and that hitch pins fit their holes snugly and securely. Check the tires' condition. Used tires are available cheaply, so there's not much reason to keep tires that threaten to blowout or lose air regularly. Match the tire size on all four wheels to keep the wagon running level. Check the air in tires regularly. Check that the deck is securely fastened to the running gear. A regular safety check will ensure the wagon is in the best shape for handling heavy loads in a way that's safe for your employees and for your crops and equipment.

Lubrication. Check if there are grease points on your wheel hubs or in the steering linkage, or if the wheel bearings take grease.

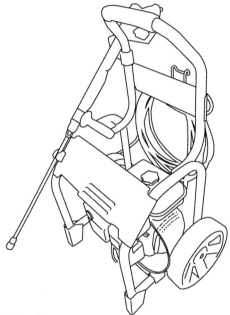

Pressure Washers

Small pressure washers can be electrically powered, but more power-ful units usually have four-stroke gas engines. Pressure washers are useful for cleaning and scouring, as when sanitizing implements between fields or harvest containers between uses. Carefully read their directions—this machine works at very high pressures, which can be as much a hazard to you as to the machine itself.

Turn on your water supply and hold the gun's trigger down before starting the engine, letting the water flow through until all air bubbles seem to have worked their way out. This is priming the pump—without this action, air bubbles may get trapped in the lines and the pump may burn itself out. Because the pump is water-cooled, do not let the unit sit idling for more than a minute without discharging; otherwise, without fresh, cool water, the pump can overheat and damage itself. Also, after turning off the pressure washer, hold the trigger down and discharge the small remainder of pressure in the line.

Common maintenance routine

See the chapter on regular maintenance for engine care and troubleshooting.

Safety check. Check over the pressure hose for leaks or wear-spots. Check that all quick-connect fittings are attaching securely. Check that the gun's trigger moves freely without sticking.

Change pump oil. The pump housing itself is filled with oil, separately from the engine's oil reservoir. This oil must be changed just like the engine oil: the first change is quite soon (around 50 hours of use), and then usually every 200 hours after that. Check the manual for oil type and grade, as engine oil will not work in the pump housing.

Troubleshooting

Engine is running, but water comes out inconsistently. check that the pressure washer is receiving full flow from the input hose. Are there kinks in the hose? Did you prime the pump? Try turning off the pump and holding the trigger on the gun. Keep holding it for at least a couple minutes: if the water sputters, there are air bubbles working their way out. Keep holding the trigger till the stream is continuous, then try starting the motor again.

Otherwise, if the engine quits suddenly when you pull the trigger, it may be a matter of letting the engine warm up before putting much demand on it. Run with the engine half-choked for a bit, discharging the pressure a couple times a minute, and let the motor work up to operating temperature before you turn off the choke all the way.

Brief Introduction to Tractors

Four-wheel tractors are not the only method for pulling field implements, but they are the most prevalent means in American agriculture today. There is plenty to know about tractors if you will be working with them or near them, but I will only offer a short introduction here. Reading or browsing your tractor's manual is recommended even if the tractor is older, as the manual can fill you in on how best to make use of your tractor's many features and apprise you of safety features and hazards.

The power rating of tractors can be deceiving if you are comparing it to your automobile, due to the way that power is managed and directed. Even a small, 10-hp or 15-hp tractor can do a fair amount of

work, or conversely a fair amount of damage, and all tractors demand respect and care for this reason.

The gearing on a tractor usually involves many different forward and reverse gears, often split into various **ranges**. This enables the tractor to match the engine's optimal power output (usually where the PTO rotates at 540rpm) to various ground-speeds, so that the operator can choose that speed most appropriate to field conditions without sacrificing power.

Tractors are often-times expected to perform tasks at steady, plodding rates, for which reason most tractors' primary throttle is the **hand throttle**. The hand throttle can be set at the desired engine speed and left in place, leaving the operator to pay more attention to other aspects of guiding the work. However, other times it may be more appropriate to be able to vary the throttle, as when driving between fields or turning around—for which reason many (but not all) tractors also have a **foot throttle**, like the gas pedal on a car. If the PTO is engaged, though, be careful about using the foot throttle—highly variable engine speeds can wreak havoc on the implement.

Most tractors are fitted with both **foot brakes** and **parking brakes**. Both systems should be functional all the time—as this is a relatively inexpensive system to keep in good order, there's little excuse to ignore faulty brakes. That said, engine braking in tractors is much more effective than in automobiles for slowing the vehicle down. This is due to the high-torque gearing of a tractor. Simply lowering the throttle can often reduce tractor speed from a charge to a crawl, depending on how much weight you're towing behind you. It is not recommended to rely solely on the brakes to slow down—so don't shift into neutral or ride the clutch as soon as you want to brake. Throttle down and only depress the clutch when appropriate, when you're at a good speed to shift gears or the engine is about to stall. The combination of brakes and engine braking is your safest, surest bet on stopping or slowing quickly, while maintaining the life of the clutch.

Do not ride the clutch. *Riding the clutch* means holding down the pedal for longer than necessary. The clutch itself is a big, expensive part which can only be replaced by pulling the tractor completely apart, and it wears out easily when mistreated. Mistreatment can be habitual or it can be occasional, so be vigilant.

If you want to stop the tractor, a natural inclination might be to hold down the clutch as soon as you brake. Much better practice is to make use of engine braking: first drop the throttle while pressing the brake pedals—this will slow the tractor. *Then* press down the clutch and stop. Do not press the clutch for more than a moment while rolling—shift into neutral or into a more appropriate gear, and avoid engaging the clutch pedal for longer than it takes to shift. Don't rest your foot on top of the clutch pedal—even light pressure can be enough to cause excessive wear.

If you find that, in order to start moving from a stop, you must *feather* the clutch (that is, linger slowly on the pedal to avoid stalling the engine) then you should start in a lower gear.

It will take practice to be able to operate the clutch quickly without jerking the tractor around, but it must be learned. Avoid hauling wagons or other implements with passengers until you're steadier on the clutch. (Really, the safest thing is never to carry passengers.)

The **differential lock** does exactly what it says—locks the mechanism which allows the tractor's wheels to spin independently of each other. The function of a **differential** is to allow a vehicle to smoothly navigate a curve—which requires the outside wheel to turn faster and cover more ground than the inside wheel. However, if while driving one tractor wheel is caught in mud or loose sand, the differential allows that wheel to spin freely and prevents the tractor from gaining traction. The differential lock forces both wheels on an axle to turn synchronously, often enabling a tractor to free itself or pull through a slick spot. The differential lock does render the tractor's steering virtually useless, though, so the lock should be disengaged whenever it's not necessary and should never be used on the road.

Four-wheel drive is available as an option on most modern tractors. **Two-wheel drive** is common and less expensive. The added traction of four-wheel drive enables those tractors so equipped to pull much greater draft in field work. Often times you will see an implement's power needs described in terms like, "Requires 75hp for two-wheel drive tractors, 60hp for four-wheel drive." Four-wheel drive tractors still have differential locks, and may have locks for both front and rear differentials separately. Generally, the four-wheel drive should be engaged only when necessary, so as to improve fuel economy, longevity of the mechanism, and maneuverability.

The **three-point hitch** is the modern standard for rear tractor hitches. This is the means by which most implements are attached and controlled. The **side links** or **lift arms** are raised and lowered by one or two hydraulic cylinders controlled from the tractor cockpit. The height can often be adjusted according to either a **draft control** or a **position lever**. Draft control responds to the amount of resistance which the tractor senses in pulling an implement, and the tractor will, within bounds, raise or lower an implement to try to maintain a consistent draft. This function is most critical to plowing. The position lever, on the other hand, simply raises or lowers an implement according to its absolute position.

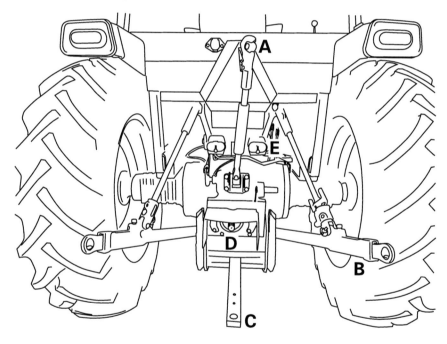

Rear tractor view: A. top link; B. lift arm; C. drawbar; D. PTO; E. hydraulic remote ports.

The **drawbar** is a more simple hitch, which simply attaches by means of a single pin. Except for pulling or pushing action, the drawbar itself has no ability to raise or lower a trailing implement. Often-times if raising and lowering action is needed for an implement at-tached to the drawbar, the implement will hook in to the tractor's hy-draulic system to power its own hydraulic lift cylinder.

Three-point and other styles of hitches are available both front- and mid-mount, and while these hitches are very useful and becoming more prevalent, they are still uncommon in North America.

Hydraulic remote ports are often placed near the three-point hitch (and elsewhere, depending on the tractor and its application) to make hydraulic power available to implements. There are innumerable applic-ations of hydraulics on farm implements, but the most typical applica-tions make use of lifting or sliding parts with cylinders, or turning axles with motors. The flow of hydraulic fluid (and thus the transmission of power) to these ports is controlled by **hydraulic remote levers** in the tractor cockpit. When lifting implements or operating remote hydraul-ics, there should be no squealing. If there is squealing, a sound of struggle from the hydraulic fittings, consult a mechanic as soon as possible to avoid damaging your system.

Electrical power is sometimes made available via an outlet at the rear of the tractor, usually as 12VDC from the tractor's own electrical system. Even in the absence of a factory-installed outlet, power for electrical parts can be easily drawn from the battery via custom wiring.

The **Power Take Off (PTO)** is the most direct means of transmit-ting large amounts of power to implements. The PTO itself is a splined shaft in the center of the three-point hitch linkage (though there may be PTOs for front- and mid-mount hitches, as well). An implement's PTO shaft then attaches to the PTO and locks in place. This shaft is driven by rotary motion from the engine, which is then converted to serve just about any purpose imaginable—driving mower blades, tilling tines, vacuum pumps, spraying pumps, fertilizer spreaders, and so on. The standard speed of PTO shafts is 540 rpm, usually clearly demarc-ated on the tractor's tachometer. As such, most implements are de-signed to operate at 540 and only 540 rpm. Almost all implements warn of the dangers of exceeding 540 rpm. Many implements can be operated at lower speeds, though less optimally or with less efficacy. The PTO should only be started with the engine *completely at idle*. Double check your throttle, hand and foot, before engaging the PTO to make sure you're idling. Starting at a higher speed will put a heavier burden on the **PTO clutch**, shortening or ending its useful life. The same way that inconsistent, unsteady throttle can jerk your tractor around, highly variable throttle will also jerk an implement's working parts around. Try to work the throttle smoothly or just leave it in one place while the PTO's engaged, to avoid damaging implements.

Note: Some tractors may have a PTO that runs at speeds higher than 540 RPM. One common alternative is the 1000 RPM PTO. These PTO shafts usually have different spline patterns to prevent a mismatch of ratings between tractor and implement, but always double-check when working with older or specialty tractors or implements.

Tractor Safety

Here are a few standard guidelines for safety in tractor operation. These items are a good place to start, but a textbook alone is no substitute for good hands-on training. Every potential tractor operator should be given direct personal instruction by an experienced operator in tractor safety. Beyond that training, every operator has to remain attentive every second of working with a tractor. You'll have to feel out what safe operating feels and looks like, using your own foresight and your own best judgment. Avoid situations that carry unnecessary risk to yourself or others.

Tractor work can be very rewarding—it's a lot of fun when it's new, and there's great satisfaction from easily accomplishing a lot of good, efficient work. To keep the work as enjoyable and sustainable as possible, it's best to learn and practice safety from the very start. All of these guidelines should apply to any tractor driver, as well as to any other worker on or near the tractor or its implements.

First and foremost, be aware of your body and its relationship to the machine. Avoid staying in uncomfortable, strained positions for very long, or you'll sustain serious repetitive strain injuries (*e.g.*, 'tractor neck'). Use cushions or props to make your seat comfortable, and position the chair so you can reach all the controls comfortably. Be aware that all tractor seats can be replaced, and the cost of comfort is very little compared with the cost of chronic pain.

Maintain control of your tractor at all times. Drive across slopes with any weight on the uphill side. If you must climb a steep slope, do so backward; if you must descend a slope, do so forward, and in low gear. Never park on an incline. Never freewheel or coast down a slope, as you may not be able to stop. Plan ahead to be in the right gear for ascending or descending, so you don't have to clutch mid-slope and potentially lose control. Even on a level surface or a road, always drive at a speed at which you can maintain complete control. Keep left and right brakes locked together on the road, since hard braking to one side at high speed can risk upset. Avoid driving near ditches or embankments, as this ground can shear away under the weight of equipment. Use as wide of a wheel setting as you practically can, as this will reduce the risk of overturn. If your wheels are set narrow, exercise special caution to avoid upset.

Avoid over-exerting yourself when working with machinery, especially mounting implements. Even the biggest implements can often be mounted with ease when done correctly, so if something is taking excessive force, rethink how you're doing it. It's often a matter of relieving tension in the linkage—that is, making sure that lift arms are neither pushing down or lifting up on the pins—that makes it easy to remove a pin or slide a lift arm. The top-link's screw mechanism can help with this, as turning it one way or another can often free up the other hitch points. Work with gravity, as you'll never want to work against the weight of machinery. Always ask for help when you need it, no matter the inconvenience.

Wear clothes that fit well to avoid getting caught in or dragged along by equipment. Avoid clothes with holes or tears. Tuck your shirt in, keep your belt close, tie your shoes tightly, and tie up or remove whatever else is hanging off of your person—watch, hat with drawstring, sweatshirt with drawstring, and so on.

Asthma and allergies are one of the principal occupational hazards of farming, so if your tractor is throwing up a lot of dust but doesn't have a cab, try wearing a dust mask. There are rubber/silicone reusable masks which are more comfortable for frequent use.

Avoid starting the tractor from standing on the ground—even if the tractor has safety switches, it's safer to just start the tractor from the operator's seat.

All contemporary PTO shafts come with plastic guards to help prevent entanglement injuries. When a limb or article of clothing gets caught around a PTO, one of two things can happen: the limb is removed, or the whole body is wrapped around the shaft. To avoid either of these situations, PTO guards need some care to stay effective: this means 1) taking care not to break them, and 2) keeping them in place, on the shaft they're designed to protect you from. The guard should remain stationary and not revolve with the shaft inside. Take a moment to learn how they work and how their grease-point access holes are placed. Guards are replaceable if broken. PTOs are one of the main sources of major agricultural injuries and deaths, so follow all safety guidelines from tractor and implement manufacturers on their operation. Note that older PTO shafts may not have guards, so give them a wide berth while they are running. These shafts can be replaced with modern guarded shafts, if desired.

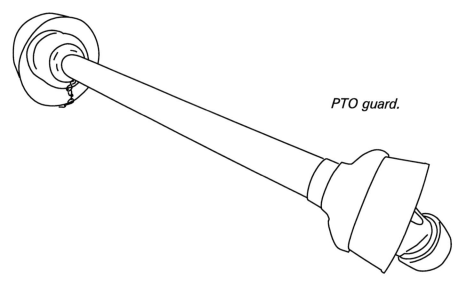

PTO guard.

Likewise, stay away from other rotating or moving parts. If you're operating an implement, disengage the PTO before leaving your tractor seat. Always turn off the PTO before working around the three-point hitch. Don't operate dangerous implements near by-standers: turn off the PTO if you're raising a revolving implement into the air in the direction of others. Mowers, tillers, and so on can shoot rocks and debris hundreds of feet if not guarded.

It should be obvious, but it bears saying: never reach into a machine while it's running. Turn it off first.

Always set the parking brake when stepping off a tractor. A runaway tractor is a serious hazard, so never chase one unless it's to save other people.

Never carry passengers, especially children. There is only one safe spot to be on a tractor, and that's in the driver's seat. Avoid carrying passengers on wagons. Never rely on people to support a load on a wagon: it's dangerous for the people and usually insufficient to secure a load, so use straps.

Never crawl under an implement or vehicle held up by the tractor's hydraulics alone—this applies to the rear hydraulics as well as any front-loader or mid-mount hydraulics. These systems can fail, or control levers can easily be knocked by accident. Use jack stands or some sturdy, solid prop to prevent crushing injury or death. Place jacks and stands on hard, solid, level ground, preferably concrete. Set the parking brake and set chocks behind the wheels.

Death from tractor roll-over was a significant problem earlier in the twentieth century, which resulted in the development of the **Roll-Over Protection Structure (ROPS)**. This consists of a U-shaped bar extending above the operator's seat, designed to bear the weight of the tractor in event of a roll-over and reduce the risk of a crushing death of the operator. If the ROPS is removed or lowered or if a tractor doesn't have a ROPS at all, there is no roll-over protection—this can be a serious hazard, so avoid driving on uneven ground or lifting unsteady loads. However, the ROPS

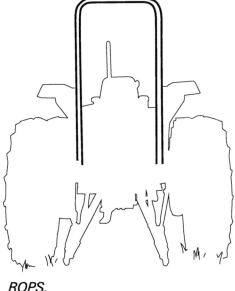

ROPS.

can only protect an operator if he/she is wearing a functioning seatbelt. If your tractor does not have a ROPS (or the ROPS has been removed or lowered), do not wear a seatbelt, as you must be able to flee the tractor in event of a rollover. The ROPS and seatbelt combination is no guarantee of safety or survival, however, so caution and best judgment should always guide the operator.

Also, to prevent backward roll-over, only pull or tow from the tractor's drawbar. This is the lowest point on the tractor, set below the main axle to prevent the front-end of the tractor from coming off the ground. When pulling or dragging, always start slow—if the rear wheels can't move forward, they will start lifting the front end off of the ground. This is how tractors flip over backward.

Almost all tractors have lights, usually a combination of warning lights, turn signals, work lights, and headlights. When driving on roads, take great care to let drivers know you're there, but avoid blinding them with high-mounted headlights. Reflective **slow-moving vehicle (SMV) signs** may also be required by local highway regulations.

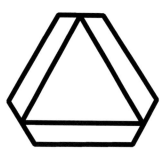

Never bypass the regular ignition wiring. If a safety switch is worn out and inhibiting ignition, have it fixed immediately. Don't underestimate how dangerous it is to start in gear.

Good safety practice may feel like an inconvenience—but remember that all these standard practices have come about after a history of injury and loss of life and limb. Look past the immediate annoyance, and avoid joining the ranks of the unlucky farmers who have been disabled or killed. It's a difficult and sobering experience when anyone on the farm receives a serious injury.

Regular Maintenance Tasks

Many of the tasks which are most important to a tractor's working well and staying in good shape are fairly routine. The tasks may be unfamiliar to you, but tractor manuals have detailed directions on all regular maintenance and serve as an excellent starting place. If you lack confidence about any particular task, don't use that as an excuse to postpone service—ask for help.

The outline that follows is for general reference only, and individual tractors can vary widely in their service intervals.

Every time you use a tractor

Do a visual inspection, checking for leaks underneath or near fittings.

Be sure to release the parking brake before you drive off, to avoid wearing out the brakes.

Check the oil. If it's below the top of the ideal range, top it up to the full mark.

On a diesel tractor, use the glow plugs (or other heating mechanism) to warm the intake air if it's 50 F or below. If it's very cold outside, let the plugs run for a good little while—our tractors range from a maximum of 20 seconds to a full minute, so check the manual. The right amount of warmth will let the engine turn over readily, rather than chugging and spewing smoke. Then let the engine warm up for a while at idle before putting a load on it—the hydraulic fluid becomes quite thick at low temperatures, and the hydraulic pump is strained by pumping the cold oil.

If you're mounting an implement, check that the side-links on the three-point hitch are level (or as out-of-level as you want them to be).

Weekly

For any tractor fluid, if you're regularly finding the level low by more than a bit, this is cause for further investigation. Look for leaks or consider other possible avenues of fluid loss—blow-by, head gasket leak, leaky hydraulics on an implement, etc. None of these fluids do you want to leak in your field or the surrounding environment.

Check the coolant level, both in the overflow tank and in the radiator (only when the engine is cool and off). Top up as needed—if your tractor has a functioning overflow tank, add the coolant there.

Check hydraulic/transmission fluid level, top up as needed.

Check water separator. If there is significant water or sediment inside (consult manual for direction), drain the separator.

Empty dust collector on air filter, if applicable. Clean outer air filter.

Check tire pressures and wheel bolt torque.

Monthly

Check radiator hoses and clamps.

Clean battery terminals.

Check belt condition and tension.

Check play in the clutch and brake pedals.

Lubricate all grease points, more often as needed.

As directed

Change engine oil and oil filter.

Change fuel filter.

Change axle case oil, differential case oil.

Change hydraulic filter(s) and/or oil.

Clean or replace primary air filter—cleaning usually means beating it lightly or (preferably) using an air gun until it gives off little or no dust. Your manual will tell you if the filter can be cleaned, and how often it should be fully replaced.

Replace the secondary air filter.

Use an air gun or a garden hose with hot water to clean the dust and debris out of the radiator fins (especially whenever an engine has been running hotter than it should).

Flush and replace coolant.

Adjust the clutch and brake pedal linkages to the proper amount of free play.

Appendix A:
Outline for Safety Discussion

I. Communication is the most important element of safety in a workplace.

    1. Communication begins with direct employee training.

    2. Every employee who works near equipment is affected, so all employees should be well-informed regarding protection from hazards.

    3. Everyone must communicate with each other about safety: if there is a hazard, or a vehicle which shouldn't be used, mark it clearly for others to see. Use flags, tape, or signs, then still spread the word about the problem.

    4. If you become aware of a problem or an unsafe condition, immediately talk to your supervisor about it so that something can be done.

    5. Keep an active dialogue among all equipment-users, so that everyone is on the same page.

II. Planning is the next element of safety.

    1. Always think ahead and consider your method. Are you creating unnecessary hazards for yourself?

    2. Avoid backing yourself into a corner—never undertake a task unless you're sure you can stop at any time if it becomes unsafe.

    3. Work with natural movements and mechanical advantage whenever possible, and avoid straining your body. Work at a natural height. Always ask for help when injury is possible.

    4. Clamps, vises, jacks, sawhorses, and other shop accessories

should be used to help with unwieldy loads. Use these tools so that you will never have to saw, hammer, or grind anywhere near your limbs.

5. Time your work appropriately. Coordinate with others to minimize injury or hazards to by-standers.

6. Use lights to improve visibility in your workspace. Keep your workspace clear and neat, to prevent other objects nearby from becoming hazards or limiting your free movement.

7. Never push tools beyond their safe working limits. If you're adapting a tool for an unintended purpose, exercise caution.

III. Safety gear and personal protection are insurance against common hazards.

1. The right clothing will prevent minor cuts and abrasions, as well as entanglement or dragging injuries. Wear sturdy, full-length clothing. Keep shirt tails and belts and other loose items tucked in or tied up. Wear sturdy boots and keep them tied.

2. Other safety gear should fit and be comfortable, so become familiar with it and find ways to be comfortable. Order the right size for all users. If you're a regular user of protective gear, consider the more comfortable re-usable options.

3. The full line-up of personal safety gear includes:

    1. Dust masks for particulate

    2. Cartridge respirators for VOCs

    3. Impact-resistant glasses or goggles

    4. Foam earplugs or earmuffs

    5. Chemical-resistant rubber gloves, sturdy work gloves

Safety items to have near work areas include:

    6. Eyewash bottles or station

    7. First aid kit

    8. Fire extinguisher

    9. Spill absorbent

10. Orange hand cleaner for grease and oil

4. Be aware of the limitations and ratings of safety gear, and replace gear when necessary. Keep it clean, and store it where it will stay clean. The right gear will be a minimal intrusion between you and your work.

5. Keep good habits and wear safety gear whenever appropriate. Long-term, gradual injury to eyes, ears, lungs, and skin can be hard to notice or care about, so follow safety guidelines carefully.

6. Respect other workers' right to safety, and warn them when your activities might create a hazard for them, so they can protect themselves.

IV. Work with respect for the farm environment.

1. Almost all vehicle fluids, oils, and fuels are hazardous to the environment and need to be contained. No grease or oil or fuel should ever touch any food. Never use a container or tool that has touched or held poisonous chemicals to handle food, and always wash your hands thoroughly before handling food.

2. Prevent leaks by keeping equipment well-maintained.

3. Prevent spills by planning: always have a container ready to catch fluids.

4. Save waste fluids and dispose of them properly. Some private businesses, as well as town or county waste disposal sites accept used oils, antifreeze, and so on. Never dump fluids on the ground or into waterways.

5. Use spill absorbent to soak up any accidental spills. Be prompt.

6. Oil- and solvent-soaked rags can spontaneously catch fire, even without exposure to flame. Dispose of them with care, separately in a metal trash can.

7. Batteries contain heavy metals and should be recycled, never thrown away.

V. General guidelines for farm safety.

1. Always be alert.

2. Avoid rushing or multi-tasking, as these distractions can quickly make an unsafe situation worse.

3. Don't be afraid to follow common sense: turn off engines before working on them. Never crawl under a poorly supported implement or vehicle—always use jack stands in good condition. Use parking brakes and chocks to prevent a vehicle from rolling away.

4. Keep safety mechanisms and placards all clean, clear, and working.

Appendix B:

Working with Fasteners and Threaded Fittings

Reference tables: Bolt size to wrench size

Many people assume that a "¼-inch bolt" takes a ¼-inch wrench. This assumption is incorrect, unfortunately, as a bolt is referred to by the diameter of its *shaft*, but the bolt *head* is what the wrench grabs. These tables will help you match the bolt's nominal size to the proper wrench size, and vice versa. So, for example, a ¼-in. bolt takes a 7/16-in. wrench.

Bolt diameter	Head and wrench size	
	standard hex bolt	heavy hex bolt
#6	1/4"	
#8	1/4"	
#10	5/16"	
#12	5/16"	
1/4"	7/16" or 3/8"	
5/16"	1/2"	
3/8"	9/16"	
7/16"	5/8"	
1/2"	3/4"	7/8"
9/16"	13/16"	
5/8"	15/16"	1-1/16"
3/4"	1-1/8"	1-1/4"
7/8"	1-5/16"	1-7/16"
1"	1-1/2"	1-5/8"
1-1/8"	1-11/16"	1-3/4"
1-1/4"	1-7/8"	2"

Bolt diameter (mm)	Head and wrench size (mm)			
	ANSI/ISO	DIN	JIS	DIN/ISO Heavy Hex
4	7	7	7	
5	8	8	8	
6	10	10	10	
7		11		
8	13	13	12	
10	16	17	14	
12	18	19	17	22/21
14	21	22	19	
16	24	24	22	27
18		27		
20	30	30		34/32

ANSI - American National Standards Institute. *ISO* - International Organization for Standardization. *DIN* - Deutsches Institut fuer Normung. *JIS* - Japanese Industrial Standard.

About threads on fasteners and fittings

There are many different sizes and specifications for screw threads. If two parts have different types of thread, they should never be fitted onto each other.

In North America, most nuts and bolts are sized according to the Unified Thread Standard (UTS). Any metric fasteners (mostly originating from other parts of the world) are most likely sized according to the ISO metric screw thread standards. All these standards define the dimensions of the thread as well as their **pitch**—how tightly the threads are packed together along the shaft. Most nuts and bolts have either **coarse or fine threads**, referring to the two most common pitches, one with fairly wide threads and one with fairly tight threads. Fittings and fastener parts are specified as male or female depending on whether their threads are **external (male)** or **internal (female)** to the part.

Standard bolts and nuts have **straight thread**, which means that the shape and size of the thread are constant along the length of the fastener.* So if you have a bolt with a matching nut, you will be able to spin the nut all the way up and down the bolt's length freely, barring any dirt or malformation. Various **washers** (flat, locking, or otherwise) or **lock nuts** are used to keep bolted joints tight. Otherwise, straight-threaded fasteners are prone to coming loose from vibration and wear.

The alternative to straight thread is **tapered thread**, which increases in size along its length. The most common application of tapered thread is plumbing parts of the **National Pipe Thread (NPT)** standard (commonly referred to as just "pipe thread"). Pipe fittings which are designed to carry liquid or gas must have a tight seal at all joints, and tapered threads make this possible by locking very tightly into each other. A **threading compound** or **thread tape** is necessary to guarantee against leaks and to ease later disassembly.

Be aware that all sizes for pipe thread are *nominal* only—for example, a 1/2-inch fitting is much wider than half-an-inch. The actual sizes are just an industry convention specified by the NPT standard. Because of this difficulty in sizing parts, many fittings are engraved with their nominal size. If you must determine a fitting's size but it is blank or too corroded to read, compare it with other parts of known size. Handy thread sizing guides are available, some for free download from the internet.

A good thing to know is the very slight difference between **garden hose thread** (straight thread, coarse) and 3/4-inch pipe thread (tapered thread, slightly finer). Because straight thread forms an imperfect seal

---

* Galvanized fasteners have a slightly different size of thread, so be sure not to mix galvanized and standard nuts and bolts as they are not compatible.

by itself, garden hose fittings seal together using a **rubber or plastic gasket** inside the female end. Pipe thread seals without a separate gasket. The two thread types are *not* interchangeable and one type does not effectively fit onto the other. If you have a garden hose or garden hose part that you would like to match to standard NPT plumbing parts, you must use an **adapter**. These are readily available from irrigation and plumbing suppliers—for example, male garden hose (GH) x ¾″ male pipe thread (mpt). Keeping a handful of these adapters in inventory is key to morale on the farm.

Loosening frozen fasteners

One of the most common problems on the farm is a frozen fastener which must be loosened or removed. Here I will mention a few of the options for dealing with a recalcitrant nut or bolt.

First, be sure you're using the right tool for the job. A loose wrench can permanently ruin the shape of bolt heads and nuts when applying significant force, so pay close attention. Using a metric wrench on a SAE (imperial-unit) fastener will not do, nor a SAE wrench on a metric fastener. A socket or the box-end of a wrench will give you a much more positive grip than the open-end of a combination wrench or an adjustable wrench. Never use toothed wrenches (such as Vise Grips®, pipe wrenches, or Channel Locks®) on nuts or bolts, unless you're willing to ruin the fasteners for re-use *and* burn a bridge if your choice of wrench doesn't work.

You will get greater leverage on a fastener the longer the wrench you use. So you will have greater effective force with a 12-inch-long wrench than with a 6-inch-long wrench with the same size socket. As mentioned in the tool section of the text, you can use other items fitted over the end of the wrench (such as other wrenches, or pipes) to extend the handle of your wrench, and this method will generate large amounts of torque for dealing with stubborn parts.

Another option is to use an impact wrench or impact driver. These are power tools (the former usually air-driven, the latter usually electric) which incorporate a hammering action into their turning motion, generating great force. Use ear protection with these tools.

Lubrication is important—douse a seized part in a penetrating lubricant such as WD-40® or PB Blaster®. Allow a minute for the lubricant to penetrate as much as it will, then try again to loosen the frozen part. You may also leave a small part sitting in diesel overnight.

Another option equal to lubrication is heat. A torch or heat gun (or, in some cases, hot water) will cause parts to expand. Think about which part must expand in order to free up the joint (usually the nut) and concentrate the heat on that part. Depending on the temperature of your heat source and the size of your parts, you may need a few minutes of applying heat or just a few seconds. Be sure to wipe off any excess lubricant before applying flame, and be safe with your heat source.

If none of these methods works on its own, try combining methods. Often times old bolts will just shear right off under high enough torque, but if they persist, you should consider cutting them yourself. You may use an angle grinder with a cut-off wheel, a demolition saw, a hacksaw, bolt cutters, or even an air-chisel.

If you're trying to remove a bolt or screw that has sheared off inside a blind hole, your best option is a **screw extractor.** Drill a hole in the center of the broken shaft, then insert the screw extractor into the hole. Use a wrench to turn the extractor to the left, which will bite into the broken shaft with its flutes and draw the broken shaft out.

Cleaning and repairing screw threads

Many nuts and bolts end up with marred threads. This condition may be due to rust and corrosion or just physical destruction. A bolt which has been bent has little hope of being fixed and must be replaced. Other threaded parts may have some hope, although repaired threads will never be as good as the original. Any threaded parts critical to a machine or implement should be replaced completely if they're damaged.

First, assess the threads in question. If two parts aren't threading onto each other easily but the threads all look fine, then you may have mis-matched thread types. On the other hand, if a few of the threads are a little flattened or ground-away, you may be able to fix that.

Once you've found the problem, choose the right tool to fix it. If the part has straight thread, you can use a thread repair tap or die of a matching size and pitch. These parts thread together with the damaged part, but they have cutting edges to remove obstructions to the threads and flutes to allow metal chips to fall away. Be sure that you're threading the tap or die straight and true onto the damaged fastener, or you will cut new thread where it doesn't belong, ruining the part. Use cutting/tapping oil to help preserve the cutting edges, and back up every half-turn or so to remove the metal chips.

Thread repair kits also contain special files to clean out threads. Simply choose a file according to its pitch—setting a file up against any undamaged threads on the part will let you quickly see whether the two pitches match. Another possibility is a triangular file, which would reshape one thread at a time, provided its edge were fine enough to fit between threads.

If your damaged part has tapered threads, it will be harder to repair. You may use a small triangular file to fix small imperfections. Otherwise, it may be necessary to recut the threads back over the original threads. Take care to line up with the original threads exactly and not wander out of plumb. Use cutting/tapping oil and move slowly, backing up every half-turn to remove the chips. And, of course, be sure to use a tapered tap or die.

Once you've done your repair work, assess the part again. Is there enough thread left for it to function safely and hold securely? For just about any fastener that will be exposed to vibration and wear, almost all the threads should be in good, new condition. If you're not sure, just find a replacement part.

Appendix C:
Maintenance Logs

These sample templates are available as spreadsheet files from the website to modify for your own use.

In a binder or file folder, each piece of equipment should have its own detailed record of services, leaving out only the routine checks and cleanings:

Equipment service record

International 574 Tractor

Date	Initials	Hours or Miles	Service	Notes
4/25	JM	11 494	oil + filter	Milky – head gasket leak?
			new front tires	
5/30	JM	11543	head gasket replaced	
			head resurfaced @ Cowan	

In that same place, I like to keep photocopies of the maintenance schedules, as well as a list of fluid grades, filter part numbers, and tire pressures for all equipment. Having all of this information in one place makes maintenance much more pleasant and preserves the actual manuals from oily hands. I also have made maintenance checklists for individual machines which integrate their service schedules (shown on opposite page). On these forms, the hour- or mileage-reading is written into the box when a service is done. Then one can quickly look back at when the last service was performed and see when it is next due.

On a clipboard or in another easily-accessed placed, you might want to keep a separate checklist for the most frequent maintenance checks: oil level, transmission/hydraulic fluid, tire pressure, coolant. Even if each check is not performed each week, you will have a handy, easy-to-read record of when checks happen. This checklist can be pretty compact, so you should be able to fit a number of vehicles/machines all on one page.

If you only have a few pieces of equipment, a one page checklist and one binder might be enough. If you have a fair amount of equipment, make separate pages and separate binders for different classes of equipment—small equipment, vehicles, tractors, etc. Keep different machines' records and data sheets separated by dividers. The less information crammed into one place the easier the management will be.

As with all record-keeping, it will require diligence from everyone involved to keep good, useful information. On most farms it's a struggle to stay on top of maintenance at all, so find a balance where record-keeping eases your burden, rather than becomes a burden itself.

Ford 1710 Maintenance checklist

Write hours and initials when check is performed.

Item	Action	Hour Reading of Service (with Initials)			Schedule
Transmission oil	CHECK	1294 JM	1380 JM →		50 hrs
Final reduction oil	CHECK				50 hrs
Tires	CHECK	→			50 hrs
Battery condition	CHECK				50 hrs
Clutch pedal	ADJUST				50 hrs
Fuel filter	DRAIN				50 hrs
Lubrication fittings	LUBE				50 hrs
Steering linkage	LUBE				50 hrs
Front wheel spindles	LUBE				50 hrs
3-pt. linkage	LUBE				50 hrs
Mid Rockshaft	LUBE				50 hrs
Rear Rockshaft	LUBE				50 hrs
Pivot shaft	LUBE				50 hrs
Clutch pedal	LUBE				50 hrs
Brake pedal	LUBE	→			50 hrs
Engine oil	CHANGE				100 hrs

Item	Action	Hour Reading of Service (with Initials)			Schedule
Fuel filter	CLEAN	1294 JM			100 hrs
Air cleaner element	CLEAN	1380 JM			100 hrs
Fuel injection pump oil	LUBE	✓			100 hrs
Fan belt	CHECK	✓			200 hrs
Engine oil filter	CHANGE	✓			200 hrs
Fuel filter	CHANGE	✓			200 hrs
Brakes	ADJUST				200 hrs
Steering free-play	ADJUST	←————→			200 hrs
Transmission oil	CHANGE				300 hrs
Hydraulic oil filter	CHANGE				300 hrs
Final reduction oil	CHANGE				300 hrs
Front wheel bearings	LUBE				600 hrs
Fuel injectors	ADJUST				600 hrs
Valve clearance	CHECK				600 hrs
Coolant	CHANGE				every year
Air cleaner element	CHANGE				every year

Appendix D:
Further Resources

Online:

The Farmer's Library
www.thefarmerslibrary.com
    I'd first like to direct you to the website for this volume. I plan to provide an expanded list of resources there, as well as my own reference material. This will include sample spreadsheets for record-keeping, a glossary of mechanical terms, and so on.

UGA Biological & Agricultural Engineering Extension Program
http://www.caes.uga.edu/departments/bae/extension/pubs/
    Has a long list of publications and articles available for download. Of particular interest might be "What Size Farm Tractor Do I Need?"

University of Missouri Extension Publications
http://extension.missouri.edu/main/DisplayCategory.aspx?C=32
    Offers a variety of useful short articles, some of which are available for free download, including G1960, Safe Tractor Operation.

Farm Hack
www.youngfarmers.org/practical/farm-hack/
    Part of the National Young Farmer's Coalition, Farm Hack promotes discussion of building and modifying farm tools. They host events, and their website features active forums and a blog.

Wikipedia
www.wikipedia.org
    Has a large amount of good background information on technical topics, often with links to outside sources. If you don't know what a word means or how it relates to your task at hand, look it up.

Core Historical Literature of Agriculture
chla.library.cornell.edu
From the Cornell library system, this archive of digitized books on farming is free to browse. Plenty of information that can be useful today, if you can find it amid the heaps of old extension publications.

McMaster-Carr
www.mcmaster.com
This industrial supply catalog can be pricey, so check around with other catalogs before you buy. However, as a high-quality source for information about materials and off-the-shelf parts, few other catalogs or websites come close. Their print catalog includes a sizing chart for NPT fittings.

Grainger
www.grainger.com
Another industrial supply catalog, with slightly different offerings, but a more product-based and less informative website.

In print:

It is unfortunate that many of the best agricultural books are not widely available at public libraries. Some of these books are widely available, or one of your farmer or extension friends might be able to lend one to you. These books often go in and out of print, but they are often available used.

Used Farm Equipment: Assessing Quality, Safety, and Economics, 1987. NRAES, $10, 34pp.
This volume gives clear guidelines in assessing farm equipment for sale.

Sustainable Vegetable Production From Start-up to Market, Vernon Grubinger, 1999. NRAES, $38, 268pp.
Vern Grubinger's book was where I started, and it remains a valued reference. There's a lot of well-researched, practical information here to provide a solid background for farm work. Includes good case

studies and interviews with individual farmers, as well as a few handy reference charts. Includes descriptions and illustrations of equipment used for different field activities, as well as a brief discussion of acquiring equipment.

Steel in the Field: A Farmer's Guide to Weed Management Tools, Greg Bowman, 2001. SARE, free online, 128pp.

A SARE publication covering mechanical weed control (cultivation). There's a lot of good information here, although the resources are getting out-of-date. The book is written for farmers of all scales, so the information is not as detailed as it could be. That said, this book is the main source for information on cultivation in print.

Farm Machinery and Equipment, Harris Pearson Smith, 1929-1964. McGraw-Hill, ~$30, 528pp.

This book was printed and updated through the 1960s, so individual printings may vary in content. Good information on equipment of the era, so there is better technical information on mechanical cultivation and small-scale tillage equipment than is available anywhere else today. Loads of other useful topics. Highly recommended, available at libraries and for purchase used and recently reprinted.

How to Diagnose and Repair Automotive Electrical Systems, Tracy Martin, 2005. Motorbooks, $25, 160pp.

An automotive guide is probably the closest a farmer will get to relevant information on electrical problems. Small-engine electrical problems are very straightforward in comparison to those on a car or truck, but the principles are the same. Tractor electrical systems are very similar to automotive systems, though there are quirks to farm equipment—some electrical problems are much more likely on a tractor than on a truck. This book covers electrical basics, then focuses on the use of troubleshooting using continuity testers, multimeters, etc.

Farm Power and Machinery Management, Donnell Hunt, 1955-present. Iowa State University Press, $40, 365pp.

At the very least, contains a good discussion of farm equipment for tax purposes, drawing the distinction between depreciation as far as the IRS is concerned and depreciation as far as the farm accountant is concerned. This book is written primarily for large-scale grain production, so it offers an interesting look into a particular type of management of a particular type of equipment. However, unless this perspective is one you're very interested in, I would not recommend *buying* the book.

Welder's Handbook, Richard Finch, 2007. HP Trade, $12, 160pp.

General introduction to welding for the novice, covering all welding processes. Includes a discussion of purchasing the right equipment. Widely available used for just a few dollars.

Repairing Your Outdoor Power Equipment, Jay Webster, 2001. Delmar Cengage Learning, $45, 368pp.

A nice introduction to the workings of small engines, with detailed information for troubleshooting and repairing. This book would be a good follow-up to the present volume, if you want to better understand engines of any size.

How to Keep Your Tractor Running, Rick Kubik, 2005. Voyageur Press, $15, 160pp.

One of the very few books available on tractor maintenance, this book is not a full repair manual. Written for the small farmer or hobbyist, with lots of color photos, organized into tasks and projects.

Index

Trademarks

Image Credits

Acknowledgments

A sincere thanks to Kristen, Rebecca, Greg, and Phil, for finding time amidst the farming to read over a manuscript. Most of all, a special thanks to Ona for tolerating all these book-writing shenanigans.

About the Author

Jon Magee has worked for Atlas Farm in western Massachusetts since 2009, after working on small vegetable farms in Pennsylvania and in Missouri.

In 2012, he founded The Farmer's Library as a technical resource for small farmers. Future projects will include guides on a variety of equipment-related topics, as well as a more expansive website. Feedback and project proposals are warmly welcomed online, at **www.thefarmerslibrary.com**.

Thanks for reading, and have a good season.